# MY LIFE
# IN CAPITALS

## BERLIN 1941 TO LONDON 1962

Astrid Thompson

© Astrid Thompson

The author has asserted his right to be identified as the author of this work in accordance with the Copyright, Designs and Patents Act 1988.

First published in 2022

Cover art, design and layout:
Nicola Thompson, Culver Design

To my children and
my children's children

'The period you grow up in and mature in always influences your thinking. This in itself requires no self-criticism. What is more important is how you have allowed yourself to be influenced, whether by good or evil.'

VÁCLAV HAVEL

# CONTENTS

| | |
|---|---|
| Prologue | 9 |
| The War Years 1941–1945 | 25 |
| After the war, back in Berlin 1945–1947 | 38 |
| Winter 1946–1947 | 52 |
| Starting school 1947 | 60 |
| Berlin Blockade, June 1948–May 1949 | 69 |
| Prisoners of war return 1949–1950 | 83 |
| New flat, new school 1950 | 93 |
| Adolescence, Spandau 1953–1959 | 106 |
| Leaving Berlin 1959 | 121 |
| An au pair in England 1959 | 133 |
| First boyfriend 1959 | 144 |
| Physiotherapy 1959–1961 | 160 |
| Leaving Berlin 1961 | 167 |

Oma 1954, age 72

# PROLOGUE

## WOLTERSDORF

My grandchildren call me Oma, which is German for Grandma. I like that for two reasons: it appeals to my vanity and self-importance to have my own special name, rather than just the usual old 'Granny' or 'Nan', but I also like it because my own grandmother, my favourite grandmother, was called Oma by all her grandchildren. When she died in 1957, at the age of seventy-five, I was fifteen years old, and I have regretted ever since that I didn't ask her about her life.

My Oma was a small woman, fairly stocky, strong and firm in body and mind. When I was ten, I was about as tall as she was. She was perpetually busy – feeding and cleaning the rabbits and chickens, collecting the eggs from underneath the fruit bushes, tending the vegetable plots that covered the entire garden and picking the berries, plums, apples and pears and storing them for the winter. She dug up and peeled potatoes and root vegetables, picked and shelled peas, kneaded the bread, made jams and sauces and just about anything out of beetroot – from beetroot cake to beetroot wine. There was white currant Schnapps, and blue plum Schnapps too, all bubbling away in large, spooky glass containers with connecting glass tubes, arrayed together in the dark part of the cellar where the huge round washtub stood, with its open-mouthed cavity for the hot embers.

It was quite a palaver to fill the tub with bucketloads of water, patiently kindle a spark in the grate underneath, and eventually get a fire going that would slowly heat the water above in readiness for the dirty linen. But if a friend happened to call in, Oma would drop everything, take her apron off and warmly welcome the visitor. The fire would go out, the water would get cold, and the dirty linen would lie in the stagnant water until the arduous procedure was repeated the next morning.

I was not allowed in the cellar, except on one occasion when Oma led me down the narrow wooden ladder and took me to the potion that would 'magic away' the warts on the back of my hands. Whilst applying some greasy substance, she murmured special spells in her dark, melodic voice, pronouncing the consonants most accurately and lingering on the open vowels as she always did. I didn't realise until much later that she wasn't really German; she had grown up in Estonia, and Estonian and Russian were her first languages. Whether or not it was because I fully believed in her boundless capabilities, the wart treatment worked – albeit only after a few weeks.

I never saw her going to the shops; neither can I remember ever seeing her cleaning or tidying the house. On the contrary, she created a huge amount of additional chaos. In order to earn some money for the family, she sewed and mended clothes for other people. Her hand-operated sewing machine stood between two rickety metal beds in the little bedroom behind the kitchen; here she produced huge piles of offcuts and scraps that lay all over the floor and hung off shelves along the damp walls.

I loved my Oma, although she never really played with us, my older brother and me. Nor did she let us 'help' in the kitchen or lick the cooking spoons or pots when she had finished with them – not that there ever seemed to be much left to lick on them anyway. She didn't really cuddle us either, but I remember sitting very close to her or putting my head in her lap when she read us a story. She lovingly tended to our head lice, scraped knees, runny noses, insect bites and the stuck-together eyelids that were apparently caused by spiders during the night. Whenever we had a problem she would instantly stop what she was doing, gaze at us with her sparkly, heavy-lidded eyes and make 'it' all better.

My brother and I spent most holidays and many weekends after the end of the Second World War with our Oma in that little cottage in Woltersdorf, just outside Berlin. The fence at the bottom of the garden was, in fact, Berlin's city boundary. The property belonged to the county of Brandenburg and the woods on the other side of the fence were part of Berlin. It was the border between the Russian zone (part of Germany) and the Russian sector (part of Berlin), and a lot of the time was patrolled by rifle-carrying Russian soldiers. But not always. It probably depended on the changing circumstances of the Cold War.

During the Berlin Blockade from 1948 to 1949 we could not leave West Berlin at all and did not see Oma that year. At other times, things seemed quite relaxed. When there were no soldiers patrolling the border, we could go into the woods and pick young stinging nettles, mushrooms and sorrel for Oma. We could climb the mulberry trees and play in the large bomb crater that had patches of soft, whitish-yellow sand but was partly filled with disgusting household rubbish and dangerous-looking rusted metal objects. As we were hidden from sight in the engulfing, bowl-shaped crater, we tended to play 'doctors and nurses' there with children from the neighbourhood.

Sometimes some of my cousins stayed at Oma's as well. Their parents would drop the children off, issuing specific requirements and instructions about sleep patterns and potty training, then leave just as my own mother had done because she had to get back to work.

It was almost a two-hour journey from where we lived in Berlin to Woltersdorf. We had to change trains (*S-Bahn*) twice and would eventually arrive at Rahnsdorf where the 87 tram was waiting at the terminus to take us the last bit of the way through the woods before it went on to the church in the centre of the village. The smell of unpolluted, chlorophyll-laden air drifting through the open-ended tram used to make me feel quite lightheaded and giddy with anticipation. Just after we passed the unstable wooden hut where the Russian soldiers hung out waiting to board the tram and inspect it, the woods thinned out and gave way to white-stemmed birch trees lining sandy paths. There we would get the first glimpse of our grandfather sitting in splendid isolation on a rickety folding chair on a lush patch of grass amongst the birch trees, pipe in the corner of his mouth, carefully turning over a page of the large newspaper on his knees. Lotte, our beloved snow-white goat, would be tethered to a long rope, grazing next to him.

My grandfather came from West Prussia, which is Poland now, as did most of his ancestors. He was a very tall, handsome man, well over six feet, though he liked to mention with a self-satisfied grin that he was the shortest of his three brothers. There he sat in the woods, a picture of peace and tranquillity, the bulbous dome of his hairless head shining in the sun, his closely shaven chin and immaculate handlebar moustache, which would have done the Kaiser proud, giving his face dignity and character. I didn't like his moustache very much because it tickled rather unpleasantly when you turned your face away quickly to avoid a hearty wet kiss on the mouth. I usually managed to make the kiss land on my cheek instead.

Saying hello to Lotte was easier. I would put my hand on her hard forehead and feel her push playfully against it with the two protuberances that were smooth-edged horns under her soft skin.

Then I would throw my arms around her neck and bury my face in her white, pleasantly musty-smelling fur whilst she tried to nibble and lick at my bare arms and legs. For a short while there were two boisterous kid goats as well. They had two bell-shaped furry white wattles hanging beneath their chins, just like Lotte, for no other purpose than to look cute.

Opa (German for Grandpa) was a man of few words and measured gestures. Maybe I would have given him an equally passionate greeting as I gave Lotte if I had been aware that he was my father's father; that he had been through two world wars and lost his two eldest sons (including my father) in the second one not so long ago. But during my early childhood there was no talk about relationships, about the past, about those who were no longer with us.

Opa would walk Lotte home before it got dark in time for Oma to milk her and for him to take his place at the head of the table for dinner. After the modest meal, when my Oma had applied his ear drops and eye drops and had cleared away the starched linen napkins and little silver cutlery benches where we had to rest our knife and fork during dinner, Opa would gently remove the large walnut leaves that were lying on the big veranda table to dry. He would spread a green felt cloth meticulously across the table, bring out the set of pre-war dominos, and shuffle the smooth black pieces fastidiously across the cloth with his large, elegant hands. Whilst Oma was clattering around the little kitchen or working at the sewing machine in her bedroom, we sat down with our Opa for a quiet, grown-ups' game of dominos, propped up on several cushions so that we could survey the table properly.

Whenever he could lay down the piece showing a four and a blank, he invariably said, '*Der Führer geht mit'm Blanken,*' which I interpreted as dialect for 'here we have the four with the blank bit'. It wasn't until much later that I realised that this respectable man was having a wayward little dig at Hitler and saying, 'The Führer's walking about with his bare arse showing.'

On Sunday mornings, my grandfather wore his pre-war three-piece suit with the gold-plated chain, attached to the pocket watch in his waistcoat, highly visible. His handlebar moustache was particularly well-waxed and trimmed. He would pack his pipe skilfully with some of the dried walnut leaves, add a pinch of real tobacco from a silver cigarette case, and put the pipe in his trouser pocket together with a box of matches. Then he would stand by the front door, hat in one hand and the pocket watch in the other, exclaiming in his deep, booming voice, 'I'm leaving in five minutes.'

At that point, all hell would break loose. Oma wasn't dressed yet and couldn't find her Sunday shoes and the black hat with the delicate lace. We would hear the frantic footsteps of her daughter, my Auntie Helga, dashing to and fro on the floor above. Helga lived in the attic – the only room on the first floor – and she worked at the post office from Monday to Saturday, so enjoyed a little lie-in on Sunday.

When Opa put on his hat, picked up his walking stick and announced that he was leaving right now, I naturally put my trust in him and my little hand in his as we began to walk slowly towards the tram stop and the impending, never-ending church service. His wife, daughter and other grandchildren would follow at varying distances and in varying states of dishevelment and panic. But the tram driver could always be relied upon to slow down enough, or even to wait, for the breathless female members of the family.

I don't know what was the worst part of this church service for me. You weren't allowed to climb around the altar and play aeroplane with the cross like we did back home in Berlin in the bombed-out church down by the canal. Instead, you had to sit for hour after hour like Opa, absolutely straight on the hard, cold wooden bench without fidgeting. It was a bit like sitting next to Opa at the dinner table, where he would take it upon himself to correct our table manners. To this day, I don't dare put my elbow on the table at mealtimes, half expecting a large hand to come across and grab my wrist to slam the elbow down so hard that it brings tears to my eyes – all, of course, without wasting a single glance in my direction nor causing the slightest interruption in the adults' conversation.

Perhaps the worst bit at church, however, was the singing of hymns. I have a suspicion that the vicar especially chose the Lutheran hymn of Psalm 130 when he saw us coming (*'Aus tiefster Not schrei ich zu dir'* – 'From deep affliction I cry out to you'). He always made a point of asking the congregation to sing all five verses, which my grandfather did with vigour, standing tall and filling the whole church with his sonorous bass voice. That was embarrassing enough, but the really excruciating bit had nothing to do with his enthusiastic singing; it was the words of the very last line: *'Wie groß auch sei der Schade'*, which means something like 'However great the harm may be.' As our surname was Schade, it could also be understood to mean, 'No matter how tall Mr. Schade is', and he was indeed extremely tall. Absolutely everybody in the church would turn round and look at Opa, nodding and smiling, and he in turn would take surreptitious little bows in all directions whilst giving his moustache a slight twirl before resuming his seat.

By profession, Opa Schade was a land overseer, a profession he'd had to acquire because his eldest brother was the sole inheritor of the family estates and the titles that went with them. A land overseer is something like an estate manager with a practical knowledge of animal husbandry. Opa had learnt to farm on a huge scale, including keeping animals, slaughtering and butchering them. He liked to mention that the lands he managed in Estonia, and later in Latvia, were so vast you couldn't ride your horse around them in a single day.

When he ended up in Berlin with his wife and six children, after

Opa 1910, age 36 with my father Karl-Heinz

the family had spent many months in refugee camps, he went to the labour exchange to get a job – only to find that there was no demand for land overseers in a densely populated area. So, he retired at the age of fifty, at which point Oma took up sewing.

Occasionally Opa's husbandry skills came in useful. I will never forget one Christmas when the whole family – all my uncles, aunts and cousins – came to Woltersdorf. It must have been 1950 when there was a lull in the Cold War, and we could travel freely from the Western sectors to the eastern zone for a while.

The tree was up with real candles on it, filling the room with the scent of warm pine needles. Each child had to stand in front of it to recite a poem or sing a little song, and then uncles and aunts took turns at the piano to accompany the singing of Christmas carols whilst the children sat on the adults' laps. Under the tree was just one present for each child, *the* Christmas present.

Adults did not usually exchange presents, but this year they had combined their resources to buy two things on the black market. One was some real coffee for Helga, who apparently found it difficult to live without it. The smell of the coffee beans mingled pleasantly with walnuts from Opa's walnut tree. The other was a bottle of thick oil for Oma because we all knew that she couldn't go to the toilet without it. I tried not to speculate what exactly she did with it, but when she eventually died of an ileus – a complete lack of intestinal movement – I realised she used to swallow the awful liquid.

After each child had received their home-made present, we sat down to eat. I had never seen so many people around one table, and I knew each of them really well. Most memorable on this occasion was the extraordinary amount of food; there was even plenty of meat. I guessed everyone must have contributed towards the meal. I wasn't only permitted to help myself, which was most unusual, but I was even allowed to take second helpings.

When we children went down to say hello to our favourite rabbits and give Lotte a quick cuddle, her pen was empty. I caught a glimpse of a professionally stretched and pinned-up white goatskin at the far end of the shed...

It is amazing how adaptable children are if they have to be. The fact that we had eaten Lotte, and that apparently this was all right, was more astonishing than upsetting. The realisation that Opa must have killed her, and Oma must have cooked her was not an easy concept to grasp, but we just took this new information on board. Rabbits, chickens, flats, homes – even people like fathers – came and went and I didn't particularly wonder where they went or why they weren't here. What was important was the here and now, where every 'here' seemed to stretch to the horizon and every 'now' seemed to last an eternity.

Oma and Woltersdorf embodied consistency and stability not just for me but for many of the family members. She had six children, of which three survived the war, and thirteen grandchildren. When a new grandchild was born, she planted a young fruit tree, and we all knew which one was ours. Mine was the apple tree, which was lucky because we were allowed to eat the apples that fell to the ground. My brother's was the blue plum tree; we weren't allowed to touch the plums, white currants or blackcurrants because every one of them was needed for Oma's procedures down in the cellar. However, we were allowed to pick and eat redcurrants, gooseberries and even the wild strawberries any time we wanted.

Oma knew a lot about plants, herbs and medicines. A dock leaf helped ease nettle stings; honey went on insect bites and made them disappear almost instantly. The common flat weeds with round leaves that grow in the cracks of paths (greater plantain) were held in high esteem as they were much better than any sticking plaster; they healed wounds, cured fever and were successfully applied to stings and bites.

Oma said that all edible mushrooms had 'a twin' that looked almost the same but was poisonous. She used to sort quickly through the assortment we brought from the woods, muttering that the odd poisonous one in a large pot of stew wouldn't harm anyone and would, in fact, strengthen our immune systems. If only I had paid more attention to what she said and did or asked her about her past. But you don't, not as a child and not as a young or middle-aged adult either, because you have yet to understand that everyone and everything is finite.

Once there was talk about Oma having been 'home' to visit relatives and friends in Dorpat, which nowadays is called Tartu. I didn't realise that this was a very long way away, not even in Germany, and that she had travelled to Estonia, which belonged to Russia then. Apparently, Oma had met up with old friends from her time at the university. Auntie Helga told me that Oma was one of the very first females to study at the University of Dorpat although, in retrospect, I think it may have been more of a finishing school than a university in those days. After she completed her 'studies', she became teacher and governess to the children of a well-to-do landowner near Dorpat.

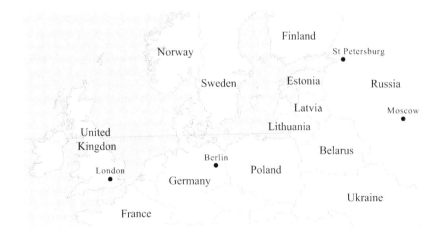

Oma (Olga Horn) as young governess

The place where she lived and worked was many miles outside town and was grandly called Schloss Tarwast (*Tarvastu mõis*), suggesting it was a stately home or manor house. The story goes that the young governess, Oma, was looking out of the first-floor window, together with the rest of the household, eagerly awaiting the arrival of the new German overseer. She fell in love at her first glimpse of the tall, erect figure of Walter Schade when he rode into the yard on his splendid stallion in the autumn of 1908.

She was twenty-six and he was thirty-four, and they were married on Christmas Day that same year. My father, Karl-Heinz Schade, was born in October of the following year.

✳✳✳

The Russians arrived in Berlin before the other Allies in the spring of 1945 and lived in Oma's house in Woltersdorf. As a three-year-old, I enjoyed the unfamiliar presence of so many handsome young men. I thought Oma was also fond of them. After all, she let them have the whole house whilst she, Opa and Helga lived in the cellar. As the house was built on a slope, one end of the cellar had a little window and a low door, which opened straight onto the back garden, so we had our own private entrance. In later years the goats, rabbits and chicken were kept there in the winter. But just after the end of the war we had no animals or eggs, as those sorts of things were much needed by the Russian soldiers.

This was a particularly happy time. My mother was with us constantly – because neither she nor Auntie Helga ever left the cellar. I found out years later that they did not dare. I had permission to go into the back garden but not to the front of the house. I remember feeling slightly naughty when I went to look at the boys who were slumped across the concrete steps by the front door, sunning themselves, drinking vodka and smoking strong-smelling cigarettes.

Oma referred to them as 'the poor peasant boys from the Far East'. She meant from the far east of the Soviet Union. They were about seventeen years old, tall and slim, grinning happily when they saw me standing there gawking at them.

They introduced me to halva, a sweet confection made from ground sesame butter and honey, which is eaten in hot countries like the Middle East and parts of Asia. I loved its stickiness and chewy consistency – but mainly its sweetness. I didn't like the vodka so much; it made me cough and feel strange.

The boys took turns to give me piggybacks and carried me around on their shoulders, making neighing sounds whilst galloping like horses. I loved it and had to hold on tight with my thighs and arms so as not to fall off. They were careful not to hurt me as I was passed

Astrid 1945, age 3½

MY LIFE IN CAPITALS

from one to the other. They carefully rearranged my clothes when they had got tangled and, whilst straightening my flimsy knickers, the boys checked occasionally that all was well down below. I suspected that was not quite right, but I rather liked it.

Unfortunately, my brother must have seen me playing with the soldiers and 'told on me', and that was the end of my little sugar intake. My mother, auntie and grandmother reacted in unison like an exploding, fuming volcano. I had never seen them so cross, at least not with me. Opa didn't get involved; he always seemed to remain in the dark part of the cellar in those days, lying on the floor on an old mattress.

Whilst playing with the Russian soldiers, I never registered in any way that they spoke a foreign language not only to each other but also to me. Recalling it now, it seems as if they clearly said things like 'try this, you will like it', and I felt perfectly comfortable chatting with them. But the day they came to our cellar door waving revolvers and heavy clubs, shouting and screwing up their faces with hatred, I didn't know what they were saying, and I called out to Oma to come quickly. Adults often talked to each other in a way that wasn't comprehensible. I knew Oma would understand and sort it out, and she did, of course.

I didn't realise until later that she spoke Russian to them. A long, heated discussion ensued. Oma stood rigidly in the little doorway. With her left hand she frantically waved us away behind her back, indicating that she would handle this, and we should make ourselves scarce, whilst her right arm was raised forward to shoulder height, palm open as in a friendly wave – or a warning not to proceed any further.

It turned out that the lads thought we had stolen their potatoes, and they had come to get them back. They had been washing them in the large white bowl in the little room right above us when suddenly a gush of water flushed them away, down a hole, down to us. They had seen it clearly and knew we were the crafty thieves. Oma had her work cut out to try and explain what a toilet was. The soldiers remained sceptical and found it hard to believe that they were expected to relieve themselves into a perfectly clean vessel in a room specially made for the purpose, and then use huge amounts of drinking water to wash away the excrement. Oma did her best to describe indoor plumbing, but it is possible that she didn't do a very good job. I heard later that when the soldiers eventually left the house, they took the taps with them because they also wanted to have magically running water coming out of the wall when they returned home.

A few weeks later we went back to Berlin, probably because Oma ran out of food and rationing coupons. I was almost four years old, and I already knew that it was important not to attract attention. Wikipedia says there were 100,000 rapes during the first few months in Berlin alone (two million in the whole country), so I am not surprised that I witnessed them quite regularly in the streets and doorways and knew to make myself scarce whenever the commotion started.

Did I understand what was happening? Yes, I did; I can't remember a time when I didn't know about these things in very accurate detail. But it was always clear to me that anything sexual was utterly private, top secret. You only shared that knowledge with other children and best friends, and *definitely* never talked about it to your mother.

The real atrocities were committed mainly by the conquering Soviet troops who were completely exhausted and had been promised a lawless period of rape, pillage and looting if they won the 'Race to Berlin' – and they did. 'Our' soldiers in Woltersdorf must have been part of the second wave, part of the occupying forces from the Siberian outback who soon went into Army barracks.

# THE WAR YEARS

## 1941–1945

When my mother went to the doctor in the spring of 1941 because she thought she was pregnant again, she found to her amazement that the doctor was far from pleased.

'What do you think you are doing, woman, getting pregnant at a time like this?' he demanded. 'The war is far from over; things will get an awful lot worse.' He was one of the very few people who recognized Germany's situation and dared to voice it – at least within the four walls of his practice.

When I was born, he just shrugged his shoulders and said to my mother, 'At least it's a girl. With a bit of luck, you may get her through.' Male babies tend to be a lot more vulnerable, delicate and frail than female babies, so the doctor thought that I had a chance of survival. He turned out to be right: the war was far from over and I survived. Apart from whooping cough, a touch of TB, scabies, and normal infections like chickenpox, measles, worms and lice, I developed healthily and happily.

My first word was not Mama nor Papa but '*Keks*' – meaning

Berlin 1939: Hermann Göring (commander-in-chief of the Luftwaffe) boasts
Berlin would never be bombed.

End of Word War II: spring 1945. Berlin Charlottenburg, the part of town
where we lived.

'biscuit'. At the first sound of the air-raid sirens, I would sit up in my cot and squeal with wholehearted delight, '*Keks!*' My mother would rush in, grab me, blankets and pillows with one arm whilst carrying the pre-packed case of clothes and provisions with the other arm. We would rush down six flights of stairs and come to a breathless halt in the cellar where all the tenants from the twelve flats in our block gathered during an attack. My father would bring another pre-packed suitcase and my brother, who is two-and-a-half years older than me.

After I was installed in a large pram, I would beam expectantly at my mother because this was showtime, biscuit time. They were the plainest biscuits you can imagine but because I never had them or anything like them during the day, their taste was the height of luxury for me and achieved the desired result: a cheerful infant, blissfully unaware of any impending doom.

The raids happened mainly during the night because bombing in the dark was less risky for the pilots, especially during the summers with their long, clear days.[1] It became difficult to get any sleep at all, so my mother, brother and I were evacuated to a healthier life in the countryside whilst my father stayed on in Berlin.

He was an electronic engineer and worked for Osram. My mother was very happy that he didn't have to join the army on account of his diabetes. Although insulin was discovered in the early 1920s, it wasn't until 1954 that the purer, longer-acting insulin we use nowadays was developed. The doctor told my father with a rueful smile that he could control the illness with a strict diet of small amounts of high-fibre carbohydrates, fresh fruit and vegetables, lean meat and fresh fish – mainly items that were hard to come by in Berlin at the time. My mother said my father lived on boiled cabbage for a while. It was one

---

[1]   After America started assisting Britain, France and the Soviet Union with the bombing in 1943, there were often several raids a night on Berlin.

of her excuses for being a rather uninspired and uninspiring cook – a trait which I inherited.

My mother, brother and I were sent to Silesia, a beautiful rural area in the south-east of Germany about twice the size of Wales, with ancient castles, rolling hills and plenty of farmland. The farmers were forced by the government to take in evacuees from the big cities and weren't impressed with my mother's complete inability to milk a few cows before breakfast or knead enough dough for next week's bread supply. She was a city girl and didn't fit in; nor did my brother. They mockingly called him 'the young prince', possibly because he spoke rather precisely, choosing and pronouncing his words carefully, a practice he had most likely copied from Oma's Baltic German pronunciation. Or perhaps they called him 'the young prince' because he didn't like to soil the nice clothes that Oma had tailored for him.

Even at the tender age of five or six, my brother avoided all rough games and dirty work. Looking like a handsome young scientist with his steel-rimmed glasses and mop of wavy blond hair, he would quietly move about the place, fastidiously examining things like matchboxes and paper aeroplanes with his nice clean hands.

So we threw him into the pigsty, the six or seven farm children and I. A huge sow was lying on her side on the soiled straw with an unbelievable number of bright pink piglets attached to the endless row of swollen teats on her belly. I had a good view because one of the bigger boys lifted me up onto the middle rail of the low fence, so that I could lean over the top. My brother was crouching terrified in the corner of the small pen with his arms around his now filthy knees, whimpering and begging to be let out.

The sow turned slightly towards him, revealing a couple of squashed dead piglets she had been lying on, and grunted menacingly whilst forcefully and melodiously relieving herself of an enormous amount of intestinal gas. We were shrieking with laughter, stamping our feet and hopping up and down with merriment.

I was two to three years old. Memories from such an early age seem to be stored like flash photographs; the recollections consist of sharp pictures completely in focus without much story relating to the before and after. I suspect a 'picture is taken' because a normal, familiar situation had an unexpected twist. What the twist or significance was in this case, I don't know.

I suspect this was one of many occasions when I ran with the mob instead of trying to help my gentle, clever brother. Or perhaps it was the first time it made me feel uneasy? That assumes, however, that a toddler has a conscience – and I don't know about that. But a toddler does have an inbuilt sense of danger, and this was possibly triggered by the event, because it definitely was a very dangerous situation – at least for my brother.

We lived on the farm in Silesia for well over a year and my recollections are all of the 'flash photography' type. For instance, there was the occasion when a new cow appeared in the cowshed. She was kept separately from the others, right at the end of a row of about ten cows. I can see myself standing in front of her, feeling sorry for her and reaching up to stroke her lips and soft nostrils. This 'picture' is kept alive because my mother filled in the subsequent events, namely her horrified reaction when I told her I had gone in to stroke the lonely new cow, the one with the metal ring through the nose and the chain around her legs. Apparently, that was the neighbour's bull, which had been brought in for breeding activities the next day. Even the farmers were scared of him and would only go near him with special handling devices.

What I find remarkable about these early 'flash-card memories' is that the photo tends to be taken from the outside and not from the standpoint of the person experiencing it. They always have to do with location and shape, with a specific depiction like, 'Here is the square farmyard, quite large with low buildings all around. I have to cross the yard diagonally from the bottom right where we sleep to the top left where the toilet is. In the middle, the wicked goose that serves as a watchdog is tied up to a post on a long rope. It is difficult to get past the hissing goose which is trying to nip my bare heels and naked calves with its hard beak.'

I am in the picture, as if someone outside me has taken it from above. I believe it is like this for most people. We tend to say 'I see myself standing / I see myself sitting / I see myself running' when recounting early memories. Presumably, this bird's eye view, this map-creating ability, is as much a part of our human survival skills as early face recognition. We seem to know about squares, diagonals, right and left, long before we know the words.

We were not the only visitors and refugees on the farm. For a short time towards the end of our stay, there was a large man with several children. He had the most awful, relentless cough and kept spitting blood into a filthy handkerchief, and his children looked pale and dirty and kept scratching themselves. They were *Volksdeutsche* (ethnic Germans) from the Ukraine, so-called 'Black Sea Germans', who had lived on the Crimean Peninsula for centuries. Although we didn't really play with them, we caught their lice and scabies, and everyone seemed to be quite cross with them about that. The fact that I also got infected with tuberculosis didn't become apparent until a few weeks later when we were back in Berlin after the end of the war. But that made me eligible for food from the Red Cross and cacao from the Americans, a privilege I much enjoyed.

Apart from that, I was very healthy and certainly look well fed in photographs. I used to sing '*Ich bin die kleine Dicke aus Zwicke*', knowing full well that most adults thought this was cute. It's just a silly ditty about being a bit plump, rather like 'I'm a pudgy, podgy pup'. From a very early age, I nearly always got what I wanted out of life – or was it that I wanted what I got? Perhaps it comes to the same thing.

I used to stand next to the farmer's wife when she was sitting at the large, thoroughly scrubbed kitchen table finishing her meal or having a snack. I would turn my bum from side to side, look up at her with my sweetest smile and sigh, 'Hm, dat does look good,' whereupon she would remove the padlock on the huge walk-in larder, cut a portion from the assortment of hard sausages hanging next to the big hams and give me a piece. My mother and brother weren't so brazen and didn't receive extra rations.

I find it hard to conjure up an image of my mother at that time, although I must have known her face perfectly well. She was the God-given centre of the universe, the decision-making force, the safe place. She was 'home' wherever we happened to be, and she was 'home' even when she wasn't physically there; it was enough to know that she was somewhere close and could eventually be found. The concept of 'mother' definitely had a particular smell and a warm, sensual component, but not a look that I can describe. Perhaps primeval love and dependency do not involve vision.

My mother was worried about my father living and working in Berlin by himself whilst she was safely in Silesia with the children. Apart from the bombing, there was the problem of getting food supplies. He couldn't queue for groceries when deliveries were made because he was at work for ten hours a day; by the time he left work, the shops were either closed or sold out.

Each time he came to see us he looked thinner. During these rare visits I wouldn't leave his side, I am told. I would hold on to his trouser legs like a relentless bulldog. When he went to the toilet, I stood in front of the door and waited patiently for him to come out again. I would sit on his lap and make up bizarre, doting terms and absurd nicknames for him with the limited but imaginative vocabulary of a three-year-old. And yet, I have no recollection of him whatsoever.

My father, Karl-Heinz Schade, age 22

There are very few photographs of my father. To me, they are of a stranger with an old-fashioned haircut – much too short at the back and sides – with dark wavy hair and round, John Lennon-type glasses. His left top front tooth had a triangular piece missing from a childhood accident; interestingly, my brother and two of my children acquired exactly the same chipped tooth in their childhoods. He looked Jewish. Not that I know exactly what that means, but my mother lived in perpetual fear that one day he would get beaten up in the streets by Hitler's roaming Brownshirts or, even worse, end up in one of the so-called 'work camps', which are now known as concentration camps.

The janitor of our block of flats, who lived on the ground floor next to the main entrance, knew everybody's business. Like all janitors at the time, he was a solid party member with special benefits and duties, and he spied and reported on everyone. He would stop my father regularly to ask him menacingly if he had joined the party yet; he meant the Nazi party, of course, as there was only one party after 1933.

Newspaper articles and reports on the German radio station were as one-directional as the one-party politics – and riddled with falsehoods. According to the media, the German army was endlessly victorious with only the odd strategic withdrawal. Towards the end of the war nobody knew what was really happening, not even people who secretly tried to listen to foreign radio stations (which was punishable by imprisonment). But there were plenty of rumours, so it didn't come as a total surprise when, in April 1945, a wave of desperate refugees arrived at the farm where we had lived for the last year or so.

The Russians were more than halfway through Poland, burning, looting and killing everything in sight, and would reach us in a couple of days. My young life didn't feel as if it were part of the ensuing panic and commotion, and I don't remember being frightened or upset in any way – but my brother does. We were caught up in the wave of shifting humanity. We were trying to get back home to Berlin, whereas the local people were fleeing westwards into the unknown, abandoning their homes, property and animals.[2]

---

[2] Within the year following the end of the war, an estimated twelve million German citizens and ethnic Germans were homeless and on the move, fleeing or having been expelled from the parts of Germany that were being annexed by Poland and the Soviet Union. Poland's borders were redrawn. Basically, the whole of Poland was shifted by one third to the west, including the population. Thus, Poland lost large territories to Russia in the east, and it gained a piece of land in the west roughly the size of England ($130,000 \text{ km}^2 = 70,000 \text{ mi}^2$), which had been part of Germany (or Prussia) for hundreds of years. Silesia and the farm where we were staying was part of this 'transfer and relocation programme'.

I don't know how many days or weeks it took to travel the 350 kilometres (220 miles) back home to Berlin, mainly on foot and by cart. I have one vivid memory of being on a train at some point – I can still see it in my mind's eye.

There is no station. We must have managed to climb the giant steps into one of the compartments. It is very crowded. The train is moving slowly and often stops for long periods, which is just as well because some people are sitting precariously on the roofs of the carriages, and through the windows I can see them hanging onto the outside of the train.

German refugees at the end of the war 1945

I sit on a stranger's lap; my mother is sitting about three seats along, on the same bench, with my brother on her lap. There is an unpleasant smell of vomit, sweat, urine and stale smoke. The floor, in as far as it is possible to see any floor between people's feet, is littered with squashed cigarette butts stuck in a layer of dark-grey slime.

I am strictly forbidden to go anywhere near that floor, which makes perfect sense to me. The nice stranger looks after me. I feel much too hot as I am wearing double and triple sets of clothing on top of each other. This was probably safer than putting the clothes in a suitcase that was likely to get lost or stolen in the chaotic crowds. The kind lady takes off several of the layers – well, basically she takes them all off – stores them in her bag and then puts my very top layer back on me again. I feel much better after that, but my mother was devastated when she found that I had 'lost' all my clothes.

There is a strange noise from outside like an approaching swarm of wasps. People jump off the roof and off the outside footholds. I can't recall what happens in the carriage at this point, I just see myself and everybody else on that filthy floor with our heads wedged under the seats. For ages our faces, hands and knees are in the stinking debris and our bums up in the air, with me wondering how this could be right.

I am unaware that the train is being attacked by low-flying, diving fighter planes, but I am aware of a new smell in the carriage, a sickly-sweet, musty smell that I instinctively identify as the smell of fear. The kind stranger is next to me making yelping sounds in the back of her throat and is being told to shut up. And then the memorable thing happens, as far as three-year-old Astrid is concerned: the woman empties her bowels into her pants. I smell it first and don't quite believe it. Surely not, not a grown-up long out of nappies? But then my ludicrous suspicion is confirmed when people shout in exasperation, 'Bloody hell, now she's gone and shit herself!'

When, as a teenager, I heard the English phrase 'to be scared shitless', I had no trouble understanding what it meant, although I didn't grasp the implications of the incident at the time. 'Poo in pants' was a very relevant, interesting and shocking occurrence to a three-year-old who was safely out of nappies, but the feeling of being scared to death by aeroplanes whizzing about trying to kill me was completely outside my field of experience and beyond my comprehension.

I believe that things we cannot relate to on some level have no meaning for us; more than that, we are simply not aware of their existence, be they killer planes or attractive boys. They only become visible to us once we are emotionally connected to them in some way.

The moment on the train and a 'flash-card memory' of crawling on all fours across a large river on a destroyed bridge that was hanging in the water at a forty-five-degree slant are the only real war-related memories I have. They are not scary because Mother was always close by. Anticipating things that could go wrong wasn't on the spectrum of a three-year-old's thinking. You took things as they came and coped as best you could, without considering the past or the future.

A psychologist may tell you that this statement says more about me now, writing at the age of seventy-five, rather than giving an accurate account of the way things appeared to three-year-old Astrid. As Albert Einstein said, 'Memory is deceptive because it is coloured by today's events.' But even if you think Einstein is right, you can't help feeling your memories are true, that they are as accurate as a video recording.

When we finally got to Berlin, my father was dead. He had died in a bombing raid whilst he was at work, squashed under his desk in his office. They shouldn't have told my mother that he had not bothered going down to the cellar during the air raids because he was too weak and tired. They shouldn't have told her that he was not killed outright, that they heard him knocking for hours under the wreckage. She felt that if she had been there to look after him and feed him properly, he would have survived. As the years passed, she consoled herself with the thought that the food shortages in the post-war years would have meant an even worse slow death for a diabetic.

His mother, our Oma in Woltersdorf, also blamed herself for the death of her eldest son. She used to pray for him every night. Although she was not a true Christian in the traditional sense, she strongly believed in the power of prayer, of meditation. But on the day of my father's death, the 24th of March 1945, she didn't pray for him because she was thinking of her second son, who had been killed in action that very same day the previous year.

Both my mother and grandmother somehow felt responsible for my father's death, but as I didn't even remember the existence of a father, I was blessedly unaware and free of the guilt that tends to assail all survivors one way or another.

# AFTER THE WAR, BACK IN BERLIN

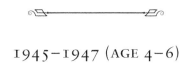

## 1945–1947 (AGE 4–6)

When my mother, brother and I got back to Berlin after the war, we went to stay with Fiene (pronounced *Feene*), a woman I had never met before. She was a tall, bony old lady with remarkably bright blue eyes under barely visible eyebrows. Her greying hair was pulled harshly back from her face and covered with a small-patterned headscarf knotted on top of her head, which made her look like a *Trümmerfrau* (rubble woman). That's what we called the women who cleared wreckage from the streets and sorted out reusable bricks.

She seemed very surprised, even startled, to see us and hesitantly allowed us to enter her small flat. 'But you can't stay here, there is no room. Where would you sleep?'

She took some clothes off the sofa so we could sit down. The floor was littered with fabric, paper patterns, scissors and pins. A Singer sewing machine stood next to what appeared to be an open window, but the window wasn't open – it just didn't have any glass. Large cardboard pieces were leaning against the wall which could be used to block up the gaping opening.

Homecoming, Berlin spring 1945

Half the living room was taken up by a huge pile of crunched up grey-green material that covered the two armchairs, the sideboard, the gramophone and the large dining-room table. It turned out to be a parachute without its harness and cords.

'It's only for a couple of days while I go and bury my husband,' my mother reassured her, 'then we will go home. I'll find a way of getting across to Charlottenburg – to our flat.'

My mother departed almost straight away and left us with Fiene. The view from the fourth-floor window was fabulous as I waved goodbye. I had never been that high up in my life and enjoyed giving myself vertigo (and Fiene a near heart attack) by sitting on the low window sill, looking straight down onto the 'rubble women' below who were clearing the pathways.

I was severely reprimanded; I was never ever to sit on the windowsill with my legs dangling outside. It was a perfectly reasonable instruction and I dutifully obeyed, but that was the moment when I suddenly knew – aged three and a half – that somehow Fiene had no authority over me and never would have; that in some unspecified but essential way I was stronger than her. It was like when teachers enter a classroom for the first time and the children take their measure in seconds, like bloodhounds ready for the kill, but equally ready to be subservient, even pleasant and loving. Something in Fiene's demeanour, body language or tone of voice made me realise that she was weak and vulnerable. She would never be able to bully me – as I felt other adults did.

We didn't stay a couple of days but for five years, from 1945 to 1950. It turned out that our home in Charlottenburg no longer existed, that everything – the piano, furniture, clothes, books, photos and important documents – had all gone up in flames.

Fiene's apartment was on the top floor of a typical Berlin block of flats with very high ceilings and tall French windows; there was a bombsite right next to it. Apart from a good-sized living room, the flat consisted of a narrow kitchen and a box room with Fiene's bed. I think the original large, smart flats must have been cut into several small units. Halfway down the staircase, between the third and fourth floors, was a functioning toilet with flushing water that was shared by several families. There was no bathroom, just a cold water tap over a small basin in the kitchen. In other words, it was all quite normal and unremarkable.

My mother, brother and I lived and slept in Fiene's front room after she had got rid of all her sewing, which had been the source of her income and independence. She spent most of her free time in her little box room, coughing and refusing to let anyone come near her. 'Germs, germs, don't touch me!' she would cry out. I can't remember her ever touching me, except perhaps tying my shoelaces and hair ribbons or making clumsy attempts to be playful by grabbing at my ankles as we went up the long staircases.

My mother didn't become a *Trümmerfrau* like most able-bodied women at the time. As she had passed her A-levels (*Abitur*), she was eligible for teacher training. The Allies insisted that all teachers who had been members of the Nazi party be dismissed. It was Catch 22: you couldn't be a teacher under the Hitler regime unless you were a member of the Nazi party, and now you couldn't be a teacher under the Allies if you had been a member of the Nazi party – so basically there were no teachers. The same applied to many other professionals like judges and higher-level civil servants. People were brought back out of retirement and prison; anyone with A-levels could start teaching straight away, receive a salary and train at the same time.

*Trümmerfrauen* = rubble-women (women clearing the rubble), my playground

From then on, we scarcely saw my mother. She was teaching full time from Monday to Saturday, attended the teacher-training seminars in the evenings, and wrote her thesis at night or on Sundays.

Those five years with Fiene (interspersed with weekends and holidays in Woltersdorf with Oma and Opa) were very happy times. I had the best childhood anyone can imagine. Like Albert Schweitzer you may say 'Happiness is nothing more than good health and a bad memory' and you may be right, but that is how I remember it.

The empty streets and the bombsites were one huge, amazing playground where I felt completely free, able to make my own choices and mistakes without any supervision. There were lots of other children and, of course, my brother Gerd, with whom I shared special thoughts and games. I felt much loved, safe and secure. Fiene was always upstairs listening for sounds of trouble, and Mother would be home sometime during the night and possibly take us to a park on Sunday, or to Woltersdorf to see Oma.

We didn't have any toys, but who needed toys with so many friends, so many games to play and such a large adventure playground? My brother didn't enjoy the street games as much as I did; he preferred to read and invent stories and intense dramas of intricate relationships and harsh morals. Old rags or bits of newspaper from the toilet represented the people. I was a necessary but totally subservient part of the performances, obediently playing several roles according to Gerd's explicit, meticulous instructions.

I was 'only a girl' (and two-and-a-half years younger), so Gerd took the lead in most things indoors. Being the boy and the elder, Gerd had to be clever at school, dependable, successful and responsible. He had to meet implicit expectations that didn't seem to exist for me. And it was Gerd who got the blame when things went wrong.

Despite occasional unexpected fits of temper, he was generally a gentle, compassionate boy. I could always rely on him to be on my side. At dinner he would eat the best things last, whereas I ate the best things first. At the end of the meal, he usually shared his saved-up treasures with me.

As I write this, I realise that playing second fiddle, yet being totally autonomous and self-contained, has been a constant theme throughout my life. I avoid taking ultimate responsibility, yet I still manage to do exactly what I like. Did the situation suit my innate temperament, or was I conditioned by early experiences? It's the well-known issue of nature versus nurture, where I increasingly tend to come down on the side of nature.

Outdoors there were practically no rules and restrictions imposed by adults, except the unspoken one that you should make yourself scarce when a woman was being molested. There was probably a rule not to venture too far from home nor too high into the ruins. But the area our gang covered was more than enough for me; I had no wish to get involved in the gang fights the older children sometimes engaged in. We were the gang from the main street, from a road as wide as Oxford Street. Three houses along from Fiene's house, the road suddenly came to an end at the point where it used to go over a bridge that crossed a wide canal. The bridge had been destroyed so the road had become a cul-de-sac, which somehow made us feel special.

We looked down on the group of children who lived in the side streets, just as they looked down on us. Business as usual in human society! Even children – or should I say *particularly* children – define themselves in terms of 'them' and 'us' based on completely absurd, contrived criteria. The sense of division between groups of people, and the propensity for inter-group violence goes back to the dawn of mankind. Time and time again history has demonstrated where that leads. But there we were, playing in the wreckage of the war that had just ended, practising the age-old skills of rivalry and division.

Our gang consisted of about twenty-five children aged from two to twelve. Although we weren't always on the street at the same time, I knew them all. I knew that they would look out for me as I looked out for the little two- and three-year-olds – after all, I was a whole year older than them. I used to take the younger ones back home if they cried, or I'd help the girls to pee in a corner without getting their skirts or underwear wet.

It seems to me now that I was on the street all day long. There were so many games to learn, to teach and to play: hide and seek; skipping with ropes; whip and top; games involving elaborate rules, rhymes and dances; ball against the wall and finger games. The favourite one was hopscotch. There was plenty of chalk in the ruins from the stuccoed ceilings that came from angels, roses and other ornamentation, and there was a patch of undamaged tarmac on the road to draw on. Not only could you design all sorts of different hopscotch patterns, you could also use the limitless supply of chalk to draw and write on the road surface. There was hardly any traffic. Perhaps once or twice a day a jeep would come along, and we would reluctantly step aside for it.

Looking back now, it is poignant to think that children in France and England were playing the same games in similar-looking ruins at that very moment. They had the same hair styles and skirt lengths, wore equally uncomfortable clothes made from flimsy parachute silk, and were afflicted with the same strains of lice and worms. Their parents listened to the same shellac records of Caruso, Marlene Dietrich and American jazz as our parents, and they watched the same Shirley Temple films and mourned departed family members and friends with the same uncomprehending misery.

Another game that we played involved a sort of catapult. We spent a fair amount of time by the canal where there were the remains of a famous department store. Fiene used to reminisce about that store and enthusiastically describe its pre-war splendour, but I couldn't imagine the plush red carpets, glittering chandeliers and lifts with lift boys in smart uniforms. It was all right to play there because Fiene could easily see as far as the canal from her fourth-floor vantage point.

There were occasionally seagulls on the canal in the early years, and that is where the catapults came in. The gulls were an easy target because they weren't flying but sitting on floating objects and picking at them intently. Yes, it was cruel, but we missed most of the time and, at best, our projectiles made the gulls flutter up for a few seconds only to land back on the drifting wreckage they were so interested in. *'Es schwimmt eine Leiche im Landwehrkanal'* – 'A corpse is a-swimming in the Landwehr Canal' we would chant gleefully and get the catapults ready.

I sort of knew that the floating objects were the bloated, gassy stomachs of the people who had said, 'If this or that happens, I shall go into the canal.' It was a common phrase. On one level, I knew the gulls were picking at decomposing human guts but, on another level, suicide wasn't a concept I understood. Our catapult games seemed no more appalling or inappropriate than climbing into people's burnt-out flats.

Other things were easier to understand once they had been explained. The bigger children obtained balloons from the chemist where you could sometimes buy black liquorice sticks and stuck-together eucalyptus sweets. These were my first-ever balloons and I was thrilled. They were very hard to blow up, were all the same nondescript colour and a bit of a boring sausage shape.

For once the passing adults noticed us, whereas normally they rushed by as if we were invisible. Some even laughed. After a few days, the chemist must have had complaints and he refused to give us any more condoms. Their real significance – in contrast to things floating in the canal – was easily understood even by the two-year-olds in our group, particularly after one of the bigger boys performed a hilarious practical demonstration on the deserted staircase.

I am not sure my mother realised that I had quite so much freedom under Fiene's supervision. Admittedly, I had to lend a hand occasionally. Sometimes I'd help carry the laundry up into the loft to be pummelled and hung on long ropes to dry, or I'd have to break off in the middle of a game and take Fiene's place in a queue for twenty minutes while she went to lie down. That often happened when the little shop in one of the side streets had a delivery of whey, one of the very few products you could buy without rationing coupons. This particular shop was in hostile territory, the area controlled by the rival gang of children. I was convinced I would be spotted as an enemy from the main street and be beaten up. But that is the sort of thing you can't share with adults, so Fiene never understood why I was clearly reluctant to help her with this simple task.

I didn't mind running a few errands for her on the Black Market, particularly when I heard that Gerd was too shy to do them. The market took place at dusk in front of the demolished department store down by the canal, almost exactly where we played during the daytime with our catapults. People would turn up and walk around casually, whispering out of the corner of their mouths 'Eggs for flour' or 'Coffee for bread'. When someone had something close to the desired swap, there was a swift exchange and they both disappeared.

Fiene used to send me there with two cigarettes, which was her week's ration. She didn't smoke but always bought the cigarettes so that she could swap them for something. I would mingle with the adults and whisper 'Cigarettes for food' a little self-consciously. I was always successful quite quickly because cigarettes were a valuable currency. Black markets were forbidden, of course, and you had to run away fast when the word went out: '*Razzia, Polente*' – 'The pigs, it's a raid'. My mother was very cross with Fiene when she found out, and I was never sent again.

Fiene (52), Gerd (7), Astrid (almost 5), 1946

It must have been frustrating for someone as organised and frugal as my mother to be dependent on a person who would happily buy lots of food at the beginning of the month when the coupons were issued and have nothing at all at the end of the month.

'They had butter in! Can you believe that?' Fiene would tell my mother excitedly. 'I bought a whole packet, and the children and I had bread with thick layers of butter all evening. Here, try.'

Not being used to such large amounts of fat, we ended up vomiting that night, and there were no coupons left for butter or margarine for the rest of the month.

Fiene would show my mother a bowl she had bought. 'They opened a shop full of china and kitchenware. When I saw this beautiful little bowl, I just had to have it. Don't you love it?' No, my mother didn't love it because Fiene had enough bowls from the pre-war years, and we needed the money for food.

You may wonder how my mother knew Fiene and what their relationship was. I didn't wonder about that at all. During the evacuation we had lived with the woman on the farm in Silesia; now we lived with this woman in Berlin. I didn't ask about adult relationships and I don't think they were ever explained. All my mother's friends were introduced to me as uncles or aunts, no matter whether they were related to us or not. When I learnt eventually that adults could have brothers and sisters it seemed very odd because, to my mind, a brother or a sister was clearly a child, not an adult.

Fiene wasn't introduced as an aunt; she was just Fiene. I never really grasped that Fiene was my mother's mother – my grandmother; it never came up until her funeral when I was twelve years old. After all, Oma in Woltersdorf was my grandmother. You don't have two mothers, so why would you have two grandmothers?

Mother and Fiene never argued in front of us children, but we knew the score perfectly well, even without eavesdropping. Mother was obviously in charge; she brought home the money and made important decisions. In retrospect, I would say she played the traditional role of a strict, overworked father, whilst Fiene played the role of the subservient, insignificant wife desperately trying to please. Whilst my mother was out all day and most of the evening, Fiene did all the washing, shopping, queuing, cleaning and cooking.

As most of the food consisted of watery soups, we had to empty our bladders several times during the night. There was a large metal bucket in the room for that purpose. I enjoyed waking up to pee because it gave me a chance to see and smell Mother lying in our bed with my brother and me and cuddle up to her afterwards. She was not usually home when we went to bed. But every now and then I would wake up to find that a candle was burning on the dining-room table with my mother and Fiene sitting opposite each other playing Halma – a strategic, addictive board game. They played obsessively well into the early hours of the morning and were giggling and intense like children. They hardly noticed me using the bucket. I would grin happily and tiptoe back to bed without the usual 'night-time mummy cuddle'. I would slip back into the spot I had just left, take one of my brother's feet and play with his toes whilst drifting off to sleep. The bed was warm with cosy contentment.

At Christmas 1946, Mother and Fiene also behaved like mischievous children. I was just five, my brother was seven. Fiene disappeared, came back as Father Christmas in a somewhat haphazard outfit and put on a deep voice that sounded rather unconvincing.

My mother started it all by saying things like, 'Oh dear, Father Christmas, you seem to have a severe case of tonsillitis, and you're so thin. Where's your tummy? Aren't they looking after you up in heaven?' (The traditional German Father Christmas comes from heaven and knocks at the front door to be let in; he does not come in a sleigh pulled by reindeers, entering down the chimney as the English Santa Claus does.) Or she would say, 'Your beard's not as lush and orderly as it used to be. Are razor blades on rations up there, too?' These things were funny at the time and rendered both Fiene and my mother speechless with laughter after a while. Gerd and I joined in, until the four of us were quite out of control with never-ending fits of giggles.

Fiene ripped off her meagre beard, wound up the turntable of the His Master's Voice gramophone and put on Bizet's *Carmen* at full volume. We rolled around the floor and danced on the sofa to the 'Toreador' song, closely followed by the 'Habanera', with an elated Fiene singing along happily in French, '*L'amour est un oiseau rebelle, que nul ne peut apprivoiser.*'

That is when I lost my Christian belief, in as far as a five-year-old has any religious beliefs at all. Somehow Father Christmas and God became muddled in my mind. I had seen very similar images depicting them; both were old men wearing big white beards and sitting on fluffy, comfortable-looking clouds. Father Christmas knocked at your door with a bag of presents over one shoulder and a *Rute* in one hand, a cane or birch with which to beat you if you had been naughty that year. You quickly sang your prepared little song, or recited the poem you had learnt by heart, assured him that you had been a good child and begged him please not to punish you – not to use the cane on you – just as you asked God not to punish you for any sins you may have committed. Not that I thought God and Father Christmas *were* the same, but they were both connected to Christmas and seemed to spring from the same book of fairy tales and myths. These were nice enough stories, I thought, but a big five-year-old couldn't seriously be expected to believe them – not now, not when Fiene and Mother had clearly shown that it was only a game.

Yet I would play along with the God game when necessary. Going to church with Oma and Opa in Woltersdorf was such an occasion. To me the church service was, and still is, a cultural event, much like going to the theatre or to the opera where you also play along with the story without believing that the actor or soprano really just died on the stage.

There is something in us, and particularly in young children, that loves notions of magic and myth. It appears to be a basic human need, or at least a necessary stage of development. Having 'done away' with the fantasy of Father Christmas and the Christian God, like others of my age I fulfilled that need with symbolic games and playing pretend.

Fiene, in her 50s

My mother, age 25, just before the war

# WINTER

## 1946–1947

The winter of 1946–1947 was a harsh one, known as the 'hunger winter'. It was the worst winter in living memory in southern England, France, Russia and northern Germany. Many hundreds of thousands died from cold, hunger, thirst and lack of strength to fight illness. There were massive disruptions of energy supplies for homes, offices and factories. Animal herds froze or starved to death, and many businesses shut down.

In Germany it was branded the time of *weißer Tod* and *schwarzer Hunger*, 'white death' and 'black hunger'. In Berlin temperatures of –30° Celsius (–22° Fahrenheit) were recorded. The situation was particularly critical in the cities. The occupying forces had imposed a rule that no international aid could be brought in. The German Red Cross had been dissolved, and the International Red Cross and the few other international relief agencies that were permitted were prevented from helping Germans through strict controls on supplies and travel.

The Allies had also enforced restrictions on the production of German steel and coal and had imposed export constraints, so other nations were unable to trade food in exchange. German calorie intake ranged from 1,000 to 1,500 calories per day, a situation made worse by severe lack of fuel for heating. Average adult calorie intake in the US was 3,300, in the UK 2,900, and in the US Army 4,000.[3] Roosevelt proclaimed: 'The German people must have it driven home to them that the whole nation has been engaged in a lawless conspiracy against the decencies of modern civilization.'[4] However, he ordered that starvation, disease and civil unrest should be limited to such levels that they would not pose a danger to the occupying forces.

Thus things were an awful lot worse after the war than during the war, but a five-year-old child does not experience the world in these terms. There is a saying that 'most misery starts with apparent happiness'. I would turn this maxim upside down for my situation during that winter – and possibly for my whole life in general – 'most happiness starts with apparent misery'.

Initially I was aware of *some* misery. For instance, most of the trees had been cut down and we needed them to play hide and seek. Even the famous boulevard called *Unter den Linden* (Under the Linden Trees) at the Brandenburg Gate didn't have any of the huge, beautiful lime trees left to justify its name. Playing on the street with other children was out of the question.

Temperatures indoors dropped well below zero, despite Uncle Böttcher from the flat below glazing the windows, which had previously been just open holes covered with cardboard at night. The dry bread we ate tasted even worse than usual; the bakers obviously mixed more sawdust with the flour than the permitted one-third. My mother had to go to hospital to have a large splinter removed from her throat; she hadn't spotted it in the bread in time. It had all been very scary because

---

3    *Consequences of German Nazism*, page 318. https://books.google.co.uk/books?id=46O Seit3bUAC&pg=PA318&lpg=PA318&

4    Directive JCS 1067

she couldn't speak to tell us what was wrong and just sat there with her mouth open like a fish out of water, pointing to her throat.

Although I was aware of these tribulations, my happiness and sense of good fortune soon prevailed because all the schools were closed for an indeterminate period. This meant that my mother, being a teacher, was home all the time and so was my brother. A happy holiday feeling took hold of me. Another blessing was the fact that the water pipe was frozen, so there wasn't enough water available for a thorough wash. The weekly body scrub in the kitchen, using a large bowl and scratchy soap, wasn't a favourite activity of mine. There was, however, enough water for drinking and cooking because, at an appointed hour, Fiene or Mother would fetch a bucket from the community pump in the street.

My mother put us to bed and told us bedtime stories. Gerd and I slept toe-to-toe in a single bed wearing several layers of clothes. Fiene put a hot brick covered in newspaper between us where we could warm our feet. This was fun. We used to rip off small bits of the wrapping and play 'postman', passing the scraps of paper to one another using nothing but our feet and toes.

In the morning we watched our breath forming white plumes of water vapour, which was great for playing steam trains and Red Indians. Gerd tried to teach me Morse code using short and long exhalations whilst holding his breath between the letters. The new window panes were covered in the most beautiful frost flower patterns in the morning. If you licked them, your tongue stuck to the glass rather painfully and you had to wait until that spot was warm enough to release it.

All that was quite gratifying and enjoyable, but the main source of happiness was the *Dämmerstunde*, the twilight hour. It tended to be a lot more than one hour due to the long electricity cuts. The four of us would sit in the small, relatively warm kitchen around the little table, sometimes with a candle on it, and the adults would tell stories and reminisce about the past. It was warm because we had a pile of anthracite that we burnt in small amounts in the kitchen stove. It was the coal that my father had stored in his cellar in Charlottenburg for a rainy day. After the flat was bombed in 1945, Fiene found it under the rubble because she knew where to look and decided to fetch it bit by bit with a small cart. She walked the seven miles from Neukölln to Charlottenburg many times, back and forth, probably under very dangerous conditions, but it meant that we were amongst the few lucky people with a room above freezing point. Uncle Böttcher and his wife often joined us for a cosy afternoon or evening in our kitchen. He was friends with Fiene and with Mother and I soon became a special friend of his, too. If I didn't cuddle up with Mother, I would sit on his lap.

During that winter, I visited Uncle Böttcher occasionally in his flat downstairs. I have no idea how old he was, but he had dark hair and a slim figure and smelt pleasantly masculine. He was of interest simply because he was a man – a rare oddity in those days! The conscription age had been extended during the final years of the war, and all able-bodied men from sixteen to sixty had been drafted into the army. They had not come home yet; they were either dead, in prisoner-of-war camps, or had escaped and were hiding somewhere. The population consisted mainly of women, children and old people.

Uncle Böttcher was the exception and had seemingly escaped the fate of most men. I don't know why he was in Berlin. He turned out to be a very friendly man and made me feel most welcome. The moment I arrived, he would send his wife into the kitchen to make me a hot drink. This was quite a long-winded affair as there were no electric kettles or gas hobs, so she was hardly ever in the room with us. Uncle Böttcher had some pre-war paper and coloured pens. We would sit at his large, heavy desk with me on his lap. With his arms either side of me, he would make a few unintelligible marks on the paper. He would add delicate lines or squiggles here and there, fill something in with heavy strokes. For a long time I wouldn't be able to make out what he was doing. Then, quite suddenly and unexpectedly, there would be a complete landscape before my eyes or a smiling, dancing Mickey Mouse. It was pure magic! I would wriggle around excitedly and give him a grateful hug and he would give me a lingering kiss on the mouth, which I didn't like at all.

Most important to me were the harmonious atmosphere and the stories I heard during the *Dämmerstunde* in Fiene's kitchen. I particularly liked stories about the pre-war years, about the ancient times before my birth when the world was completely different from the 'normal' world of 1947. I was glad I didn't live in those dangerous days when the streets were full of automobiles, double-decker buses, trams sparking electric charges, and people on bicycles trying to balance in between them. Allegedly, there were no ruins whatsoever but instead row upon row of brightly lit shop windows, some even with flashing neon lights outside. 'Where on earth did the poor children play?' I asked myself.

Then there was the problem with the bananas, supposedly a delicious, yellow, oblong-shaped fruit. People used to eat them in the street and throw the thick peel on the pavement, which was very dangerous because old ladies could slip on them and fall over. I envisioned the paths covered inches deep in slimy banana skins with elegant old ladies trying in vain to navigate through them, slipping and sliding all over the place as if they were ice-skating. With the roads flooded with traffic and the pavements full of banana skins, it was difficult to imagine where anyone found anywhere to play hopscotch in those pre-war years.

Apparently Fiene had been fat before the war (the word for 'obese' didn't exist). She had been three times the size she was now because her second husband had loved to take her to the local pub and feed her *Buletten* (Berlin-style hamburgers or flattened meatballs) to go with the beer. Gerd and I couldn't get enough of the stories from when Fiene had been extremely large. She had to describe again and again how she ate piles of *Buletten* just to please her husband. She had to demonstrate repeatedly how big her bum had been – in standing position and in sitting position – and we would all howl with laughter. I didn't know anybody who was fat – absolutely everybody was thin, except for the lady in the laundry who was simply enormous and could hardly move. You could barely see her hands and feet because her arms and legs ballooned over them, but apparently that was water rather than fat and she was actually very ill.

Occasionally a cute little mouse would keep us company in the kitchen and provide some entertainment. It would suddenly appear when everyone was sitting absolutely still, scurry across the floor and rapidly brush its whiskers along the surfaces and edges of the furniture. Then it would stop, put its weight on its hind legs, lift its forelimbs from the ground and extend its head upwards, sniffing with a twitching movement of its nose and whiskers, and surveying its surroundings with glassy black eyes. It was the closest thing to a pet I had but it was impossible to touch it, let alone catch it. Fiene laughed at my mother's endeavours to kill the 'filthy vermin'. Mousetraps were set and holes in the skirting board blocked off, but all to no avail. The mouse survived the winter in our kitchen and disappeared in the spring.

The presence of the mouse triggered tales about rats – and there were plenty of them, not only in the ruins but in the backyard of our flats and in the cellar. Fiene would recount her horror at seeing me, a few months earlier, playing with a fat, dead rat. She had never run down the eight flights of stairs so quickly. She had dragged me upstairs and scrubbed my hands and face until they were red raw.

I thought rats were quite cute, despite a friend telling me about a boy who sat in the ruins of his house every night armed with a heavy stick. He thought the body of his little brother was under the rubble and he had to fight off the rats that would come and nibble at him at night.

Prompted by tales about rats, Fiene at long last revealed, during one of the *Dämmerstunden* chats, how she had managed to grow some amazingly healthy tomatoes during the previous summer.

Many people had window boxes and tried to grow something edible in them, and Fiene had somehow got hold of tomato plants – a very rare commodity. The plants grew vigorously and produced an abundance of large, juicy, dark-red tomatoes. People spotted the robust growth 'strutting its stuff' outside our window on the fourth floor and came all the way upstairs to ask for the secret of such success.

Fiene always shrugged her shoulders and demurely murmured something about 'luck' or 'south-facing'. But when pressed hard during one of the kitchen chats, she admitted it had to do with the rats. They had chewed through a sewage pipe in the part of the cellar that was allocated to her flat. Human sewage had spilled onto the floor, and over the months had turned into something resembling manure. Fiene went down when there was nobody around and collected it to feed the tomato plants. That explained the rubber boots and bucket that were kept separately in a cupboard.

My mother had refused to go into that dark cellar ever since she had found a nest of baby rats there, together with the mother rat defending her offspring. Apparently, rats can jump as high as your throat, and they somehow know that this is the place to attack you. We all said Fiene had been terribly brave, but we were more than pleased that she hadn't told us whilst we were enjoying the tomatoes. Sometimes it is better not to examine the reason for success too closely.

When the electricity supply was on, the radio would murmur away in the background. It was always set to the *Suchdienst* (Tracing Service), which listed missing persons. From a distance it sounded a bit like the British shipping forecast, except that it went on for hour after hour. The adults would keep half an ear open listening to the announcements. With their repetitive rhythm and regular intonation, they sounded cosy and reassuring to me because I wasn't fully aware of the terrible reality behind these broadcasts.

As well as the millions of missing soldiers, there was an ongoing influx of refugees from the eastern territories; by 1950, a total of approximately 15 million Germans had fled or been expelled from east-central Europe. Countless uprooted and homeless people strayed through the country; many of them were children looking for their parents, or parents looking for their children. 'From the end of the war in 1945 until May 1950, around 14 million tracing requests were made. In 8.8 million cases, the Tracing Service was able to pass on concrete information about the fate of next of kin.'[5]

In March, the extreme cold passed. Schools and factories re-opened, and the *Dämmerstunden* in the kitchen became a thing of the past. The kitchen mouse moved out, and my visits to Uncle Böttcher became less frequent. By the summer of 1947, the Western Allies' policies had changed because of their opposition to Communism and the beginning of the Cold War.

The American Secretary of State, General George Marshall, announced that the US would make billions of dollars available to those countries that wanted to participate in the general economic recovery of Europe. In return, those countries would buy American goods and provide investment opportunities for American capital. It was noted that 'an orderly, prosperous Europe requires the economic contributions of a stable and productive Germany'.[6] Many restrictions were lifted, and West Germany was on the road to its *Wirtschaftswunder* (the 'economic miracle'), whilst I was looking forward with some apprehension to starting school in the autumn.

---

5    Quoted from https://www.drk-suchdienst.de/en/information-and-background-knowledge/
     history-of-the-grc-tracing-service/

6    July 1947: Directive JCS 1779 replacing Roosevelt's directive JCS 1067

# STARTING SCHOOL

## 1947

On my first day of school, Fiene took me firmly by the hand and marched me down the Kottbusser Damm for a mile or so. We went in the opposite direction to where I usually played by the canal and the

Astrid: back row second child from the left

destroyed bridge. This was brand-new territory for me, but I didn't see much of the surroundings because I was too busy scrutinising the pavement, trying to avoid stepping on the numerous cracks and lines. I was six years old and was indulging in superstitions and ritualistic games – not treading on the cracks was an obsessional 'must' to ensure good luck on that important day.

It was half past seven in the morning, so we were a little late for the eight o'clock start and had to walk quite fast. Understandably, Fiene became frustrated with the way I was hopping and skipping all over the place and occasionally pulling her off balance. 'Why can't you walk properly!' she complained irritably, indicating with her voice that she simply wanted to have a moan and didn't really expect her protest to make the slightest difference.

Naturally, I continued in the same vein. She didn't realise what I was doing and how important it was to avoid stepping on the lines and stay on the intact bits of the pavement, and I was certainly not going to enlighten her. It was one of those things you couldn't discuss with adults because they wouldn't understand. In truth, I couldn't discuss it because I didn't really know why it was so important – but I was sure that it would invite all manner of ill-fortune if I didn't obey this sacred ritual.

When we arrived, an older girl took me to my classroom and showed me my desk. Then all the new children repeatedly practised standing to attention when the teacher entered the room and sitting down quiet as mice when she slowly lowered her outstretched arm with the palm of her hand facing downwards. It looked a bit like the reverse of a Hitler salute.

After that, she showed us how to write an 'a' on our chalkboard. Finally, a group photo was taken in front of the most intact piece of wall (with only a few bullet holes), and we were allowed to leave. All of that had taken one hour, so the first school day was over at nine o'clock. Fiene had waited by the gate to walk me home. She informed me that the next day I would walk to school by myself.

The educational system in Germany is different from England: children only attend school in the mornings, including Saturdays. But when I started in 1947 there were not enough undamaged schools in Berlin, so two schools had to share one building. One school had the building in the morning; the other occupied it in the afternoon. They swapped sessions every week, so every second week I went to school in the afternoon.

In Berlin, you start school the year you turn seven; I was one of the youngest in my class, because I was only just six. Another important difference between British and German schools is that in Germany you don't play at school, nor do you eat; you are there simply to learn. You have lunch at home, and in the afternoon you do your homework. After school on that first day, I eagerly plastered my chalkboard (and half the pavements outside) with wobbly a's all afternoon, ready to show the teacher.

Walking to school the following day all by myself seemed like a delightful adventure. Gerd went to a different school and had already left. I set off with an eager heart and freshly plaited hair, giving no thought to the fact that the very concept of 'adventure' implies an uncertain outcome.

I had every reason to feel confident: there was no likelihood of getting lost because I just had to walk straight for a mile or so and cross lots of little side roads. There were no vehicles, so there was no danger from them. I danced across the pavement, nicely avoiding the lines and cracks, with the chalkboard covered in a's proudly dangling on a rope over my shoulder. I felt very grown up and excited and tried not to think about hostile gangs of children pouncing on me from the side streets.

Then I saw the dandelion on a bombsite I was passing. From habit, I had kept an eye open for any edible weeds growing in the ruins – like stinging nettles – for Fiene's soup pot. As I went to pick the much sought-after dandelion, a boy I had never seen before came up from the other side with the same intention. I bolted. Expectation and imagination were stronger than reality; I fancied I was about to be set upon by an aggressive gang of boys and ran for my life. I fell and badly grazed my knee and elbow; even worse, the black slate with my homework shattered into lots of little pieces.

The teacher was perfectly nice about it, but my hopes and expectations were shattered along with the slate for a long time, at least an hour or so. As there were no paper or pencils, it was imperative to have a chalkboard. Eventually I obtained another, but this one was made of corrugated cardboard painted black and always felt like a sad replacement. It wasn't like 'the real thing', and I didn't enjoy writing on it.

By the time I got home, scabs had formed on the injuries. Appropriate 'tut-tuts' were offered but no cleaning up – it was probably too late for that anyway. Bits of grit had dug into the flesh under the scabs, and the dark-coloured scars remain visible to this day. They remind me that every time you make an 'us', you make a 'them'. The 'them' and 'us' stories of warring gangs of children were probably true, to a large extent, but I had never seen these allegedly hostile gangs and had no idea what they looked like. The oldest and strongest kind of fear is fear of the unknown.

After the dandelion incident, I tried to ignore the ruins and potential food on my way to school. Instead, I invented a new ritualistic mind game to make the walk more entertaining. I imagined a long line of Astrids following me, a row of little girls identical to me. Each one had to copy my every move in sequence.

It was a bit tiring to be the head of such a long crocodile, but it was fun to imagine myself staggering on pre-war pavements through slippery banana skins and inventing new hops and twirls which the multiple Astrids had to reproduce when they came to the same spot. I occasionally looked behind me to check that they were doing it properly. I am sure a psychoanalyst would have a field day with that recollection! I sometimes see small children moving along in weird ways, and I have some idea of what they are doing. Perhaps it is quite normal after all.

Eventually I grew tired of the cloned Astrid crocodile, possibly because a difficult situation demanded my full attention. One of the burnt-out shells of the pre-war shops along the main road had been renovated, and I had to pass it on my way to school. It was a shoe shop, and above it in large, bright-red capital letters it said 'SALAMANDER'. You could not ignore it because it stood out so clearly amongst the grey, dusty surroundings.

I didn't know that a salamander is a lizard-like animal, and perhaps quite a suitable name for a shoe shop, but I knew the word only too well. We used it every day in a filthy little counting rhyme to sort out who was going to be 'it' in the next game. It was so rude and obscene that even bigger children dare not say it out loud and only whispered it. Still, using bad language was one of the joys of childhood, and Salamander happened to rhyme with *Arsch auseinander.* I have no wish to translate the offensive verse here; let it suffice to say it has to do with the *derrière.*

The problem was how to get past the shop every day, because adults would be able to see what you were thinking as you walked past the Salamander sign. Bad language and pornographic images were things adults simply didn't indulge in; I was sure that such things were completely reviled and unacceptable to them. I was convinced they didn't even understand some of the innuendo in their adult correctness and innocence.

I developed various strategies to pass the danger spot: waiting until the coast was completely clear, and then quickly running past the shop; walking backwards, attentively inspecting my bitten nails; talking or singing to myself whilst looking up into the clouds. It was a daily struggle.

The horror was complete when my mother decided to buy me new shoes – not hand-me-downs – and took me to Salamander.

'Oh no, not here,' I stammered in confused desperation, whilst a frosty sensation crept up my bare legs and my feet refused to move. Only a thin partition separated me from the ominous interior of the Salamander place.

'Whatever is the matter?' my mother asked.

Before I could summon up the strength to think of something to say, her hands gently pushed me through the door. I felt the blood rushing to my head and burning my face. I couldn't look the sales assistant or my mother in the face, let alone talk to them.

Struck dumb with shame, I wondered how the smart young shoe lady could work in such a shop. Since then, I have learnt that children are not the only ones who suffer from this type of self-inflicted guilty conscience. Adults think they can handle it, that no one can tell what they are thinking, but once you know what to look for you can see it. For example, at boring board meetings, men in particular, indulge in inappropriate 'salamander thoughts' on a regular basis.

There were forty-eight girls in my class, and we always had the same very old, patient but dull teacher. Looking at the group photograph, much to my surprise I remember most of the girls' names. Two of them had fathers at home and naturally we asked what it was like to have a father at home, what a father actually *did*. It was a bit like asking them about some exotic bird or unusual pet. They both said much the same and the answer was strangely fitting: 'He sits in an old armchair all day and just stares out of the window.'

The rest of us thought that we didn't need – or want – one of those, although it has to be said that in the coming years quite a few fathers did turn up from various prisoner-of-war camps. Some of them ended up in the canal when they found out that there was nothing to come home for.

Not having a father was the norm, and so was your mother going out to work all day. It is important for children (and adults) to feel that they fit in with their peers. Conformity may well be more important than academic achievement because the need to be part of a group is instinctive; it's a matter of survival. Anxiety and vulnerability come from thoughts of 'I'm different, I don't fit in'. We felt safe in the knowledge that our life was 'normal', that we didn't stand out from the crowd. We not only had similar home lives but also similar hairstyles, and the same itchy scalps and empty stomachs, and we shared old German customs like curtseying when you passed an adult you knew or shaking hands with every hello and goodbye.

In those post-war years, not many people upheld the tradition of presenting children with a huge bag of sweets on their first school day, but my mother constructed a *Zuckertüte* for me. This enormous, lovingly decorated, cone-shaped cardboard construction was filled mainly with scrunched-up newspaper and had a few liquorice and eucalyptus sweets on the very top on some parachute silk. It was the thought that counted. I was delighted because I had assumed a *Zuckertüte* was one of those things that only happened before the war, before I was born and therefore hundreds of years ago.

It is a custom that persists to this day and gives you an idea how keen German children are to go to school – having to be coaxed with a huge bag of sweets. I loved walking to school but not being there. In fact, I remember very little of anything that happened in the classroom, and I was very late learning to read.

I felt lucky that my desk was at the back because nobody could see if I joined in – or, more often, didn't join in – the group recitals of poems, timetables and communal answers to questions posed by the

Astrid starting school, 1947

teacher. I simply imitated what the children around me were chanting. On the whole, they seemed to know the correct responses a lot better than I did, but that was all right as I didn't feel we were competing. I felt bored but safe. As I couldn't see the teacher's face from the back, I felt sure she couldn't see my face either.

As a child, you assume all people see the world as you do. Sitting in the back row, I comfortably picked my nose and bit my nails, not realising that the teacher was probably not short-sighted and could see me perfectly clearly. It was only years later that I grasped that my classmates were not really much cleverer than me; the answers to her questions were often chalked up on the blackboard, which, to my eyes, was just a foggy mess.

During break we went into the dusty schoolyard and taught each other new games, rhymes and tricks. I felt everyone was my friend and we were on the same wavelength. All interaction seemed straightforward. A question like 'Do you want to play hopscotch?' or 'Do you know the next verse of this rhyme?' received a simple, honest answer of 'yes' or 'no' and required no deliberation. But when an adult asked you something, you automatically thought 'What is the right answer, what do they want to hear?' Truth and honesty hardly came into it and giving an untruthful but fitting answer didn't make me feel the slightest bit guilty. Adults were not your 'friends' but your 'superiors'; children were clearly not a part of adult life and were expected to know their place, to do as they were told and mind their own business.

Life changed dramatically for the adults before I finished my first school year. In 1948, Berlin became the scene of intense conflict between the Soviet Union and the Western Allies. The Soviets tried to annex West Berlin and integrate it into their communist state by starving the city into submission with a blockade. The world teetered on the brink of a Third World War.

# BERLIN BLOCKADE

## JUNE 1948–MAY 1949

Mutual mistrust ruled the relationship between America and the Soviet Union – between capitalism and communism. When the US government started a massive aid programme in 1948, pumping dollars and goods into Europe to aid recovery, the Soviet Union felt threatened and prevented the Eastern European countries under their control from taking part in the arrangement.

Our relatives living in the Russian zone proclaimed that the Americans had gone shopping and 'bought West Germany' at a bargain price; they said that rebuilding Western European economies was mainly in America's own interest. But we didn't complain. As we were living in the American sector of Berlin, we now saw some improvements – brand-new shoe shops, for instance, which was very acceptable even if they were called 'Salamander'.

After France, Britain and America combined their three zones into one area (West Germany), the Russians felt even more threatened. They were desperate to show some strength and decided to harass the population of the Western sector who travelled through their territory by stopping and searching everyone at gunpoint. The journey to Oma in Woltersdorf suddenly took much longer than the usual two hours.

I remember the first extra-long border crossing well, because my mother had unravelled an old jumper and packed some of the wool and a crocheting hook to teach me how to crochet during the train journey. Gerd was sitting opposite us, reading.

I see myself bravely stabbing non-compliant wool loops with the metal hook, occasionally thrusting my elbow with fervent gusto into my mother's ribs when trying to force my fingers and wrists into unfamiliar positions. The train is slowing down and comes to a stop on the tracks well outside the next station, and the hum of the electric engine fades away. After a while, people stick their heads out of the windows to see what is happening, but they swiftly sit down again when they see a couple of Russian soldiers coming along the length of the train, locking all the doors and windows from the outside.

It is very quiet. Some people are whispering intensely to each other. I continue with the task in hand, proudly noticing the beginnings of a scarf taking shape. Gerd continues reading.

It is summer. My hands start sweating. We eat the boiled potatoes Mother had brought for the journey and empty the water flask. There is no toilet on this train. It is getting very stuffy being locked in with all the windows closed.

After about an hour, three soldiers unlock a door and climb into the airless compartment. I notice that they are not carrying their rifles slung over the shoulder as usual but are holding them firmly in their hands in front of their bodies.

'*Papiere!*' Everybody is fumbling through their bags and pockets. Rigid bodies pass identification papers with trembling hands. A faintly musty, sweetish smell drifts through the carriage. Eye contact is painstakingly avoided – with the soldiers as well as with fellow passengers. As I look around, I only meet the eyes of other small children and the stare of a soldier whose lower arms are both covered from wrist to elbow in gleaming wrist watches.

Bags are prodded, opened and any desirable contents are confiscated – shoes, watches, and black-market merchandise like hams, coffee and cigarettes. It is all handed down to a soldier waiting by the tracks with a cart. We don't seem to have anything that the Russians want but, as my mother closes the bag, the soldier waves his rifle around in an agitated way, signalling to her to come with him.

My mother wrote in her *Reflections and Memoirs*:

*When the Russian soldiers eventually came through the train to check the luggage and papers, one of the soldiers indicated to me to step outside. I have no idea why. The children stayed behind. He took me into a makeshift hut and tried to ask some questions. But his German was not really up to it. So he stood for ages silently in front of a long list of names that was pinned to the wall, which, I assume, was a list of wanted people. As the minutes went by, it gradually dawned on me that he did not really know what to do, and I began to feel less frightened. After he had pretended to study the list intently for ten/fifteen minutes, whilst glancing across towards me at regular intervals, he signalled with a dismissive gesture that I should go. Goodness me, was I relieved to be back with the children on the train again!*

I am also pleased to see her back on the train. I had not been frightened; it never occurred to me that Mother wouldn't come back in good time because she always does. Gerd, who had moved across to sit next to me, returns to his book and his bench opposite to make room for her.

The train still doesn't move. Some men discreetly relieve themselves into empty food containers or, in their desperation, simply urinate into a corner by a door. It must have either been a very long train for three or four soldiers to inspect, or perhaps the soldiers had received instructions 'from above' to delay every train as long as possible. All I know is that by the time the doors and windows are unlocked, and we start moving again, I have run out of wool and the so-called scarf is finished.

※ ※ ※

In June 1948, the situation worsened and came to a head. The Western powers decided to introduce a new form of currency in their part of Germany, which they said would help trade. The Russians protested. They interpreted this as a hostile action, a decision taken by the other Allies without their consent. They refused to permit its use as legal tender in Berlin. The Western Allies completely ignored Stalin and introduced their new currency in West Berlin on 23rd June 1948.

Berlin was located within Soviet-controlled Eastern Germany, close to the new Polish border. It was like an island, completely surrounded by the Soviet zone. The city was divided into four sectors: French, British, American and Soviet. The introduction of a strong American-backed currency in the three Western sectors would cause economic chaos in the Soviet zone of Germany and the Soviet sector of Berlin because everyone would try to get rid of their old money and change to the new currency. The very next day, Stalin cut off all rail and road links to West Berlin: the Berlin Blockade. Access to the city would be re-established the moment the 'illegal money' was removed from the city.

The West, however, saw this as an attempt by the Russians to starve Berlin into surrender and to take over – to annex – the capital.

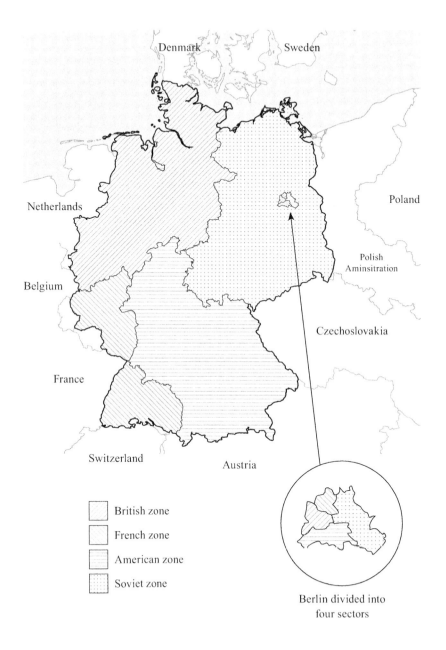

Denmark

Sweden

Netherlands

Poland

Belgium

Polish
Aminsitration

Czechoslovakia

France

Switzerland

Austria

British zone

French zone

American zone

Soviet zone

Berlin divided into
four sectors

Allied-occupied Germany during the cold war 1945–1989

Truman did not want to cause World War III. Instead of military action, he ordered a massive airlift of supplies into West Berlin, everything from food, drink, medicines and clothing to raw materials and coal.

Stalin was sure that West Berlin would soon surrender but he was wrong: the Berlin Blockade lasted 318 days – almost a year. There was an average of 1,500 flights a day (one a minute twenty-four hours a day, seven days a week, but on three different airfields) delivering 5,000 tons a day – a formidable accomplishment of organisation and discipline.[7]

My mother wrote in her *Reflections and Memoirs*:

*They provided dried food and coal for 2.5 million people. But there was not enough to go around. We had thought we knew what shortages and famine meant, but during the year 1948/49 we learnt to live also without any electricity or heating. All generators and most factories had stopped due to lack of coal... We subsisted on the flown-in potato powder, egg powder, milk powder and clarified butter (butter from which all milk solids have been removed). The nutritional deficiencies and illnesses resulting from this diet devoid of any fresh produce have never been mentioned nor researched, to my knowledge. To this day, feelings of revulsion, nausea and disgust creep over me when I think of that food. But the dread of hunger was so strong that for many years I kept a large bag of dried potatoes in the cellar, just in case.*

I vividly remember the scrambled egg made from the American dried-egg powder; I thought it was delicious. The milk powder

---

[7]  https://en.wikipedia.org/wiki/Berlin_Blockade

MY LIFE IN CAPITALS

provided the basis for all sorts of innovative, mouth-watering drinks and puddings. Frau Böttcher downstairs was particularly talented in that direction, adding mysterious sweetening ingredients to her hot-milk drinks – so I started visiting Uncle Böttcher more frequently. The new dried ingredients also pleasantly enhanced Fiene's self-styled cake, which consisted mainly of the dregs that remained after brewing coffee. These weren't the residue of real coffee beans but of a concoction of roasted acorns, chicory and grain. It is called *Muckefuck* – a corruption of French *mocca faux,* meaning false coffee. It gave Fiene's 'cakes' some bulk but very little else, so the addition of powdered milk and egg much improved the abominable slab.

Visits to Oma in Woltersdorf were out of the question during the year of the blockade as she lived in the Russian zone, so there were no fresh eggs or produce from her garden and the adjoining woods. But, due to the TB infection I had contracted in Silesia at the end of the war, I was eligible for *Schwedenspeise,* a daily bowl of soup or oatmeal courtesy of the Swedish Red Cross. You had to bring your own spoon and container which was, in most cases, a washed-out old tin. You had to eat your portion there and then; you were not allowed to take it home or share it with your brother. They also gave us a large bottle of cod-liver oil, from which my mother administered a teaspoon each to both Gerd and me once a day. All in all, I enjoyed quite a good diet and played happily on the street as usual.

When the first aeroplanes started buzzing above our heads in June 1948, we stopped playing and climbed up the nearest rubble heap to have a closer look. Neukölln, where we lived, was on a flightpath and is very close to Tempelhof Airport. The propeller-driven planes were remarkably low in the sky. We would pass on hilarious stories about some planes flying so low and at such a steep angle that their lowered undercarriage would occasionally pick up washing lines, complete with the washing still hanging from them, from the rooftops of the

Children in Berlin cheering the lifesaving aeroplanes at the beginning of the airlift 1948

four-storey buildings surrounding the airfield. We called the planes *Rosinenbomber* (raisin bombers) because as they landed the pilots threw out sweets to the children lined up on the edge of the airfield. The sweets were attached to little parachutes made of squares of paper. From a distance, it looked as though the planes were dropping dozens of miniature bombs which wafted down to earth like a cloud of dandelion puffs. We were too far away to catch any of the tiny bundles, so the novelty of watching aeroplanes soon wore off, and the continuous droning and throbbing of the engines became quite irritating and disruptive.

At night I would lie awake watching a row of planes crawling across the sky in the windowpane directly in front of my bed. They looked and sounded like fat bumble bees with luminous, gleaming eyes. There were always about five planes in the dark window opening, but from the street you could see a complete 'pearl necklace' of up to ten planes at any given time.

It was impressive how they followed precisely the same path, all entering from the right at the cross bar of the window and leaving the window on the left exactly by the knobbly bit of the window frame, night after night. How did they do that without any roads or signposts in the sky? My answer was simple: they were Americans, larger than life, from the legendary land of milk and honey, bursting out of their skins with courage, invention and know-how. Although I had never been to a cinema or seen any moving pictures, I knew these Americans were 'Supermen' with muscular bodies and unimaginable powers.

When I met my first Americans face to face, I wasn't disappointed. The American Embassy staged a Christmas party in 1948 for German children living in Berlin during the blockade and invited my brother and me. I was seven years old; Gerd was nine. The invitation came completely out of the blue; my mother's friend, Lydia, must have pulled some strings to get us onto this most prestigious list of beneficiaries. Being Jewish, she had some influential acquaintances amongst the occupying forces.

Mother took us to a station in the centre of town and we waited with some other children and parents in absolute silence, looking anxiously up and down the empty, snow-covered street. I was wearing a freshly washed bow in each plait, and Fiene had polished my 'Salamander shoes' so hard that the winter sun reflected on their shiny surface.

Eventually a fleet of black, gleaming limousines approached slowly and eerily from the left, silently pulled over to our kerb with an elegant swerve and came to a graceful stop. Several men and women ascended from the low seats, poised and gracious, while the chauffeurs in uniform stayed behind the steering wheels. We were being welcomed by dazzling white teeth, set in strong angular jaws, energetic smiles, clear bright eyes, glowing smooth skin and an aura of well-being and self-confidence.

I wasn't disappointed. These were real, flesh-and-blood American champions drifting effortlessly into our grey world like exotic birds of paradise. The men looked like athletes who had just come out of a shower and were about to step up to receive their well-deserved trophies. The ladies sported halos of wavy yellow hair; they were wearing bright-red lipstick and see-through stockings that made their long legs appear to be naked. Any German woman wearing make-up would have been classified as a tart, a girl of questionable virtue who sold her body to soldiers for a pair of nylon stockings. But I understood instantly that completely different rules and judgements had to be applied to this glamorous breed of people.

Gerd and I waved goodbye to Mother through the back window of the limousine and were whizzed off by the benevolent aliens in their beautiful, bizarre 'spacecraft'. We, and the other children in the car, sat rigidly on the beige leather upholstery, trying to hold our breath in a vain attempt not to spoil the wholesome atmosphere by our presence.

We came to a stop outside a building that looked like a Greek temple and climbed up the wide stone steps. These were nothing like the stone steps outside the church where we sometimes played; there were no steps missing – every single one was there, swept and free of snow – and most of them were intact, with only a few cracks and bullet holes here and there. The entrance hall was equally immaculate and imposing, smelling of fresh paint and paraffin stoves.

But the thing I remember most vividly is the long table set out in the middle of the huge room into which we were led. There was a row of tall wooden chairs evenly spaced along both sides. In front of each chair, a round paper plate had been placed meticulously on the immaculate white tablecloth. Each plate contained the same quantity of brightly coloured objects which turned out to be sweets, none of which I had ever seen before: strips of chocolate wrapped in shiny silver paper; multi-coloured Smarties, and round, hard fruity sweets with a hole in the middle.

Our American benefactors had a job trying to get us to sit down. We were all standing by the door, unable to comprehend that all this was for us.

To my amazement, after a short while I found that I was beginning to understand what the Americans were saying. For months afterwards I told everyone that I understood English, until my mother explained to me that the Americans had, in fact, spoken 'Pidgin German' with a heavy accent.

No doubt we sang songs and played games, but that wasn't unusual and thus not committed to memory. I think it is the unfamiliar, the unexpected and surprising events that we tend to remember. Continuous realities are taken for granted; it often is only when circumstances change that we realise that we have been living in paradise – or hell.

I will never forget the exhilaration and pleasure of peeling away the silver paper from that small bar of chocolate, my very first piece of chocolate. Nor will I forget the moment when I was told I could actually take my present home with me. Every child had been presented with a pretty parcel. Mine contained a fully dressed celluloid doll that not only had movable arms and legs, but also had glass eyes with lashes that closed when you lay her down.

It felt as if I were visiting the Queen's chambers and a guard had opened the doll's house cabinet and handed me one of the priceless dolls. It was bliss: I had been entrusted to handle the treasure, and she was all mine to play with. When it was time to go home, I naturally laid the doll gently underneath the Christmas tree and left. A young man came running after me and asked (in Pidgin German, as it turned out), 'You not like doll? You not take doll? You like car?'

He led me back into the room to the Christmas tree. The young man was no doubt astonished to see this little girl burst into uncontrollable sobs as he handed her the doll to take home.

My mother wrote in her *Reflections and Memoirs*:

*...The children had a Christmas party as never before. Food and drink as much as they liked, Christmas games and songs, merriment and happiness; and there was even a Father Christmas with presents... Astrid got her first doll... Everyone also received a jumper, a pair of socks and lots of sweets. You can imagine my feelings when I fetched the children from the place where I had dropped them and saw their bright, sparkling eyes. As was the case so often in those days: I never had an opportunity to thank those generous people for their kindness.*

The very same people who had dropped deadly bombs on Berlin were now saving our lives. They were throwing sweets to famished children and arranging an amazing Christmas party. In all likelihood, the self-same pilots who had flown the identical aeroplanes during the war were now risking life and limb to keep the *Luftbrücke* (airlift, literally 'air bridge') going. I am not sure what this says about human nature and about politics. I never put the events next to each other until now. Does our perspective change that much when we get older?

On 12th May 1949, Stalin abandoned the blockade. After eleven months of relentless air traffic, the skies (and our diet) returned to normal. Three roads connecting West Berlin with West

Air lift memorial Berlin, *die Hungerkralle*

Germany were opened, bringing lorry loads of food and all kinds of merchandise. Rationing was abolished six months later in the western parts of Germany.[8]

Fiene stopped looking like a stick insect and started putting on weight quite rapidly. She revelled in the culinary delights that she had dreamt about constantly for years: butter, bananas, bacon, cake, chocolate, real coffee. By the time she died three years later she

---

[8]   Food shortages and various forms of rationing persisted in East Germany and East Berlin until the fall of the Berlin Wall in 1989. In the UK, food rationing was only abolished five years later in July 1954.

was almost back to her somewhat bulky pre-war size. My mother's deep indentations above her collar bones, which we had called *Salznäpfchen* (salt and pepper dispensers) because they looked like those old-fashioned little bowls, started filling in again.

I saw my first bananas, and their appearance was a surprise. I expected all fruit to have a relatively round, plump shape. The taste was also a disappointment because they tasted like old potatoes that had gone off. My mother had bought one banana and opened it there and then on the street, which was unheard of; you never ate on the street. She gave a third to Gerd, a third to me and kept a third to herself. The instant she heard my whinging 'ugh' as I dug my teeth into the pulp, tasted the sickly-sweet flesh and felt the furry-dull consistency on my tongue, she unceremoniously grabbed the piece of banana from my hand and devoured it.

Although it would be another twelve years before the infamous Berlin Wall was built, the city was now (1949) divided into an increasingly flourishing West and a stagnant East. There were two mayors, two different governments (one capitalist, one communist), two very different currencies and a hard border. As the eight-hundred-year-old centre of town, with the ancient seat of government, imposing museums, cathedral and main town hall, belonged to the eastern sector, a lot of important documents were lost by the West including my mother's hard-earned teaching certificate.

I was too young to feel incarcerated by living on an island of 480km², which is a little less than one-third the size of Greater London. I didn't miss the centre of town, nor did I miss all the cousins and aunties living in the East, most of whom I was not to see again until the fall of the Berlin Wall forty years later.

# PRISONERS OF WAR RETURN

## 1949-1950

'Come and meet your uncle. Come and say hello to your Uncle Herbert.' A stranger sat at the large dining room table with my mother standing next to him, a young man with blond, straight hair, soft-looking skin and a high, round forehead like my mother's.

I curtsied, as was the custom for greeting adults.

'Oh my, she has turned into a proper young lady,' he said softly. It was 1949, and I was seven years old. 'You were a tiny baby when I last saw you.' He gazed thoughtfully into my eyes, then looked up at my mother. 'Is she allowed a spoonful of molasses?'

She nodded. On the floor next to him stood an enormous silver-coloured tin, the size of a bucket. After he had prised open the lid with a knife, he dipped our buckled teaspoon into the thick dark-brown syrup, expertly twisted off the excess drips and offered it to me. As the sticky substance hit my pallet, I fell in love – with the molasses and with the new uncle.

I was told that he was my mother's baby brother, which apparently made him a 'proper' uncle, a blood relation. Baby brother? Whatever

Uncle Herbert 1947, age 32

next! How could my mother have a baby brother? This was a fully grown man. I had never seen him before and, as far as I was aware, his name had never been mentioned. This friendly young man with the deep melodious voice, who had arrived with gifts from the gods – like a huge pot of molasses – was a baby brother?

'I brought you something from England,' he said to my mother. He bent down and rummaged around in an old army rucksack. He put two oblong-shaped tins on Fiene's white tablecloth with *SPAM* written on their sides in large yellow letters. 'And a little something for the children.'

The 'little something' turned out to be pages of cardboard with colourful prints of dolls, dolls' clothes and cars. We were allowed to sit on the floor and cut them out with real scissors, dress the cardboard dolls with the cardboard clothes, and shape the cars into three-dimensional structures.

Later that evening I lay with Gerd in our bed, feeling as if Christmas had suddenly arrived in the middle of spring, and listened to Mother, Fiene and Uncle Herbert talking until sleep got the better of me. As we all lived in one room, which served as lounge, dining room, bedroom and office, Gerd and I were used to overhearing adults' conversation while we played on the floor or tried to go to sleep. I suspect a lot of 'hidden information' about the war and pre-war years passed into my subconscious that way.

When I woke up the next morning, the new uncle was gone. It was explained to me that he had a fiancée waiting for him a few miles outside Berlin, in the Russian zone. She had been waiting for him for ten whole years (1939–1949). 'Just like a princess in a fairy tale,' I thought.

Uncle Herbert visited us regularly over the next few years, eventually with his wife, the princess. As I grew older, I pieced together bit by bit what had happened to him during the war.

He didn't talk about the war, but now I know he was fighting under Rommel in North Africa. They capitulated in 1943, two years before the war ended. Whenever I see those battles depicted in films or documentaries, I can't help thinking of him being amongst the soldiers and reflecting on how lucky he was to be captured by the Western Allies before any serious harm came to him.

The German prisoners were taken from North Africa to America on cargo ships. It took six weeks to cross the ocean. I was very impressed: Uncle Herbert had spent three years in the legendary land of milk and honey – as a prisoner of war. Unfortunately, he wasn't at all keen to talk about that, when pressed, he just said that he wanted to forget that part of his life.

He did, however, like talking about the four years he subsequently spent as a British prisoner of war. At the end of the war in 1945, the United States sent most prisoners home to Germany but those who had 'technically' surrendered to the British army, like Uncle Herbert's regiment did in North Africa, were sent to England. He was terribly disappointed not to go home like the other German prisoners, but Clement Attlee's post-war British government deliberately ignored the Geneva Convention by refusing to let the Germans return home. England desperately needed the workforce; up to one-fifth of all farm work was being done by German POWs.[9] In Uncle Herbert's case, it was another four years before he was finally released in 1949 and turned up on our doorstep.

I think he must have been placed somewhere in Cornwall or Devon. He said that at first the villagers had obviously been instructed not to have any contact with the enemy. Girls who had German boyfriends were understandably ostracised, and sometimes disowned by their families. But, to his amazement, he never experienced any hostility despite the brown uniform with orange felt patches he had to wear at all times that identified him as a prisoner of war.

He was allowed out of the camp during the day, and often worked alongside British farm labourers. People were friendly, eventually returning his smiles and waves of hello as he walked freely through the villages to and from work. Despite the language barrier, he said he shared jokes and laughter with them; he liked the English sense of humour.

When the ban on fraternisation was lifted, he was even invited into people's homes. He wrote about the first Christmas he spent with a British family: *Until the day I die, I shall never forget that Christmas Day – to be in a private home after all those years of war and captivity, invited and welcomed by friendly people.*

On one of Uncle Herbert's visits, he made me a pair of slippers. He ripped some rags into long strips of material, took three strands

---

9   http://www.bbc.co.uk/history/british/britain_wwtwo/german_pows_01.shtml

and braided them into tight plaits, then rolled and stitched the plaits together to make the shoe shape. To make hard-wearing soles, he braided old nylon stockings that were too laddered to be repaired. The whole procedure took no more than an hour.

'I made hundreds of these in England in my spare time,' he explained. 'At first, I used to go around the villages to collect rags and stockings, but later people actually brought them to me. I made lots of friends that way, and often people gave me produce from their gardens or even a piece of meat in return.'

My 'Herbie-slippers' were extremely comfortable, and I wore them for several years. I often wondered how many English housewives were walking around their English houses with the same 'Herbie-specials'.

Uncle Herbert seemed to be popular and useful wherever he went. By profession he was a baker and pastry chef, but he had developed a flour allergy when he was in his early twenties. Red-raw blotches had appeared on the skin of his hands, and he could not stop coughing. However, although he had to give up baking, he could still give advice and help willing English housewives make their dough rise better and their loaves look bigger.

I would have done anything for him, except stop biting my nails. Mother tried again and again: 'Stop biting your nails! Don't put your fingers in your mouth. Do it for Uncle Herbert.' She eventually started a regime of inspecting my nails every Saturday night and whacking each bitten finger (which was all ten, of course) with the scissors. I was used to the occasional, well-deserved smack – all children were – but this seemed rather severe. I understood, however, that it was a desperate last resort.

Everything else had failed. Gloves at night, bitter substances on the fingertips – nothing did the trick. Most children had got rid of the worms we all seemed to have in 1946, but not me. I scratched at night and kept reintroducing the parasites by biting my fingernails. In the end, the worms succumbed to the application of regular enemas but the nail-biting only became less frantic when it was no longer a source of disgrace and humiliation. 'You will never get a job with bitten fingernails. Nobody will employ such a person.' This pressure was removed when I came to England when I was seventeen and found that lots of people were biting their nails – and they had jobs.

When people ask me nowadays why I came to England, I like to say, 'For two reasons: one because you don't get ostracised for biting your nails in England, and second because you can leave the house without having to polish your shoes first.' And there is some truth in that.

It was around the time Uncle Herbert appeared in my life that I first heard about another uncle, another blood relation. His name was Rolph, and he was Oma's sixth child, my father's little brother.

Uncle Rolph 1941, age 19

When we went to visit Oma and Opa in Woltersdorf after the blockade, we were met with great excitement: a letter from Rolph had arrived! He was alive. After seven years of fruitless attempts to find out what had happened to her youngest child, and not knowing whether he was alive or dead, Oma had received a letter from him through the normal postal service, not through the authorities. The postmark on the envelope showed that it had been posted a week earlier in southern Germany.

Auntie Helga was terribly excited. Here, at last, was evidence that she had been right all along, and that her little brother had not perished in the vast plains of Russia as everyone else had assumed. She wouldn't let go of the grubby sheet of paper with her brother's handwriting on it in blue ink.

*Dearest Mother, I hope this finds you healthy and well. Spring is particularly beautiful this year, the apple trees are clad in puffs of white and pale-pink blossoms and the sun feels beautifully warm after the long, cold winter...* Then there was something about missing her and thinking of her, polite regards to his papa and finally his signature: *your loving son Rolph.*

This was absurd! It was definitely his handwriting, but why was he writing about the weather and not telling them anything about himself and where he was? Why was the writing so messy with unnecessary marks and dots everywhere?

Auntie Helga figured it out: some of the dots seemed to be placed deliberately under certain letters and, when put together, the marked letters read, *heat the paper by holding it close to a light source.* Pale brown writing appeared miraculously between the lines of blue ink on the heated paper: *A friend is smuggling this letter out of the camp and is posting it for me in Germany. I am in a Russian POW camp in Czechoslovakia. I have a plan of how to escape and shall be with you in a few months.*

Amongst the photos hanging on the wall between Oma's piano and Opa's grandfather clock was one of Rolph taken in 1941 when he was on leave, age nineteen. When he was drafted into the army at the beginning of the war, he was seventeen; when he was planning his escape from the Russian prisoner-of-war camp he was twenty-seven. As far as I was concerned, the photo had never been of any interest; it hung amongst a whole row of similar looking young men in uniform whom I didn't know. But this boring 'Rolph-photo' now turned into a photo of a possible uncle who might turn up in flesh and blood and thus became more interesting.

During the following months, I paid special attention when there was talk about Rolph – Uncle Rolph to me. In the evenings, I would lie in a dark corner of the warm living room on two armchairs that had been pushed together to form a little bed, whilst the adults sat around the table close to the huge, tiled stove. They must have thought I was asleep. Oma told my mother that Rolph was the baby she had wanted to abort in 1921 because the existing five children (and the impractical husband) were more than enough to cope with on the road and in the refugee camps, where they tended to live after World War One.

Many Baltic Germans fled from the Bolsheviks at that time.[10] Oma and Opa left their home in Estonia and made their way through the Baltic States (Estonia, Latvia, Lithuania) and Poland towards Germany. Pregnancy was the last thing Oma wanted under these circumstances, but when she went to have the abortion, the man refused to do it.

I heard Oma continue in a conspiratorial tone of voice, 'He said to me, "My dear lady, I will not kill this healthy seed in your body.

---

[10]   Russian Revolution 1917 and subsequent civil war. https://en.wikipedia.org/wiki/Baltic_
Germans

MY LIFE IN CAPITALS

You will thank me one day. God's way is not our way, and this child may well be your comfort and consolation in old age.'" Her hands trembled involuntarily as she took a deep breath and sighed. 'How right he was! Until this letter came, I thought I had lost all my four sons. Now I live in hope again.'

Every time we went to visit Oma in Woltersdorf that year expectations were high. Would there be any news about Rolph? As soon as we saw Oma, we knew the answer. She would stand in the kitchen welcoming us with a strained smile, head cocked to one side, biting down on her lower lip. Then she would clear her throat and say, 'No, nothing yet, nothing at all,' as she smoothed and re-smoothed the front of her skirt. There was no second letter, not even a postcard.

Then one weekend, about eight months later, he was there when we arrived in Woltersdorf, sitting in the downstairs bedroom by the small window. It was a total anti-climax, at least for me. There was no huge celebration, no merriment, no joyful calls of 'Come and meet your uncle'. Everyone seemed quite subdued.

When we went in to say hello, he gave monotone, one-word answers to my mother's questions and stared down at his folded hands on his lap. Gerd and I were told to go and play, but the door to his little room had been left slightly ajar so I spied on him later on. He was sitting on his own by the window with sagging shoulders, a rug over his knees and an empty Schnapps glass on the coffee table beside him. He was running his hands through his hair distractedly and muttering to himself. His lips twitched as he stared out at nothing.

How had he escaped? How had he made his way across roughly 500 miles of occupied territories without ration cards or money? I'm afraid I don't know; I didn't ask because it was none of my business – and perhaps I wasn't particularly interested once I realised that this uncle wouldn't take me swimming in the nearby lake or sit me on his lap.

I overheard Oma saying that Rolph had problems sleeping and was waking up from nightmares; apparently, he couldn't remember what had happened nor where he had been.

Years later, when I was an adult, I tried several times to talk to him about the war. He always gave inadequate answers, saying he couldn't remember or simply refusing to talk about his experiences. I never got much more than the name of a battalion or regiment, and that he was involved in horse-drawn transportation in Poland and Latvia.

A little research revealed that he was there when the 'elimination' of the Jewish and Roma population started, when mass killings took place, and Gypsies and Jewish people were being rounded up and put into ghettos. I think there is a strong possibility that he was part of that.

Later he fought in the German 6th Army in Russia and was one of the few who survived the battle of Stalingrad[11] and the Russian work camps. The widespread fear of being captured by the Soviets was fully justified, although it has to be said that survivors were still returning from the Soviet camps as late as 1956, eleven years after the end of the war, which gave lots of fatherless families cause for hope.

Over the next few years, I saw Uncle Rolph much more frequently than Uncle Herbert because Rolph lived in West Berlin whereas Herbert lived in the Russian zone. After the Berlin Wall was built in 1961, we didn't see Herbert until he was over sixty-five and retired; the East German government didn't mind their senior citizens going to live in the West and drawing their pensions there. By then he was in an advanced stage of Parkinson's disease and no longer the amiable uncle full of joy, love and laughter.

---

[11] The Battle of Stalingrad (23 August 1942–2 February 1943) is often regarded as one of the largest and most brutal battles in the history of warfare. Simply horrific to read about it!

# NEW FLAT, NEW SCHOOL

## 1950

In 1950, my mother managed to find a flat to rent in Charlottenburg near the school where she worked. It was a miracle – or simply the result of her determination and perseverance – because at the time no new houses were being built, and there was a huge shortage of accommodation in West Berlin.

The very next time Fiene complained, 'There's more than enough sewing work out there now. I could earn quite a pretty penny if only I didn't have to look after the children all the time and had my own space,' Mother interrupted her quietly with, 'We are moving out next weekend.'

Fiene broke off in mid-sentence and put a hand over her mouth. My mother feigned not noticing her profound astonishment and turned away to busy herself with the papers on her desk.

Fiene's eyes softened and grew wistful; to my amazement she looked more upset than relieved at the news. I would have liked to have given her a cuddle, but I couldn't, because I knew she still had her aversion to being touched.

So that was that. At the weekend, we put all our clothes into one suitcase, Mother's books and papers into a large bag, and took the underground to Charlottenburg.

The move marked the beginning of a new life for me, but any change, even a change for the better, is always accompanied by drawbacks. I lost all my playmates, and when I went down into the yard and onto the road expecting to find a ready-made community of children waiting to receive me and my skipping rope with open arms, I was sorely disappointed. There were no children playing in the street.

Charlottenburg is to Berlin what Kensington is to London: an historically affluent, posh area. Although war, the great leveller, had more or less wiped clean the slate of inequality, Charlottenburg still felt different from Neukölln. Here there were no unwashed children playing in the streets and women didn't drink beer in the local pub, wearing curlers in their hair.

Tradesmen and beggars regularly came into the courtyard. I had never seen that sort of thing before. Some just stood there, cap in hand, and sang something with a wobbly voice, faces raised towards the windows, hoping for some reward. Others resolutely announced their business, their voices echoing around the walls of the yard: '*Messer- und Scherenschärfer*' (knife-and-scissor sharpener); '*Brennholz für Kartoffelschalen*' (firewood for potato peelings). We only had one kitchen knife and we washed our potatoes, so had no peel to swap for firewood, but some people rushed down to take advantage of the offer. Others would stand in the middle of the yard, legs astride, and yell, '*Lumpen für Papier.*' They were collecting rags for the production of paper.

The men and women collecting scrap metal had a horse-drawn waggon. The moment we heard their calls, Gerd and I would dash downstairs, across the yard, through the smart corridor under the front building – taking the three marble steps in the hall in one leap – and out into the street. We were told to stand back, so we would just stare at the heavy, muscular animals and giggle when they relieved themselves right there in the road.

The ice-cart man came with a horse and cart and called at least once a week. That was also worth a dash downstairs in the hope of touching the huge bars of ice that were being delivered to the dairy shop across the road. People who possessed an icebox (a forerunner of the refrigerator) would go to the van and have bits of block ice hacked off, which they used to keep their food fresh.

But everybody's favourite caller was the organ grinder. This was the *Leierkastenmann* – the hurdy-gurdy man – a street musician who played a barrel organ that was operated by turning a handle.[12] As soon as the crank was turned and the pipes and bellows started sounding their synthetic, breathy tunes, windows around all four sides of the yard would be thrown open and people of all ages would lean forward onto the windowsill, swaying to the music and often singing along with the well-known songs. They were frequently songs about love and romance, but my favourite song was *Mackie Messer* (Mack the Knife). It is originally a German song with lyrics by Bertolt Brecht:

*Und der Haifisch, der hat Zähne,*
Oh, the shark has pretty teeth, dear,

*Und die trägt er im Gesicht.*
And he shows them pearly white.

---

[12] A *Leierkasten* is not really the same as a hurdy-gurdy man, but similar. They featured all over Europe from the beginning of the eighteenth century. The *Leierkastenmann* was popular until the 1920s in Germany, but during Hitler's reign they disappeared, and were even forbidden at one point.

*Und Macheath, der hat ein Messer,*
Just a jack-knife has Macheath, dear

*Doch das Messer sieht man nicht.*
And he keeps it out of sight.


*Denn die einen steh'n im Dunkeln*
There are some who are in darkness

*Und die andern steh'n im Licht*
And the others are in light

*Und man sieht nur die im Lichte*
And you see the ones in brightness

*Die im Dunkeln sieht man nicht.*
Those in darkness drop from sight.

*Leierkastenmann* around 1955

MY LIFE IN CAPITALS

It was the custom to throw a coin wrapped in paper down to the organ grinder, which his monkey or his dancing child would pick up for him. Once, I was allowed to do that. I stood well back and threw the wrapped coin furtively to the man five storeys below. He spotted it and doffed his hat, smiling up in the direction of my window. I found the situation painfully embarrassing, maybe because it felt like throwing a titbit to a performing animal in a circus.

As I am writing this, it occurs to me that there may be a connection between the uncomfortable feeling I experienced on that day and my reluctance to tip people. Why do I cringe when I observe customers at the hairdresser sidle up to their stylist and surreptitiously slip some money into their hand or pocket before leaving? I guess I feel it is demeaning for the receiver, and patronising on the part of the noble donor. Even as a child I felt it violated the assumed principle that people were equal.

In truth, all these activities in the courtyard were a short-lived residue from pre-war times; some of them were a throwback to customs of the century before. Only a few years later, the horses were replaced by engines and the 'recycling people' became redundant because standards of living in West Berlin were rising fast, thanks to American support.

We had paper and pens at my new school; only the teacher at the front used a large slate board and chalk. He was called Herr Werth (Mr Worth), and we were the first class he had ever taught. He was twenty-one years old and possessed the rare knack of making his pupils want to please him, or was it just the positivity that his name conveyed that made him so likeable?

Names and designations seemed very important to me at that time. I started playing around with nicknames for my mother. That wasn't intentional, it just happened because our relationship had shifted significantly now that we saw so much of her. 'Schalli' was my mother's name from that time until she died. It is just a sound and doesn't mean anything. She became 'Schalli' to everyone, just as her mother had been 'Fiene' to everyone.

In years to come I even introduced her as 'Schalli' to my friends and my husband's relatives in England, until she objected one day after someone thought she was called Charlie. But after I introduced her on the next occasion as 'my mother, Mrs Schade', she felt that was much too formal and she preferred the nickname after all.

Every morning Schalli, Gerd and I left home at twenty past seven after we had breakfasted together. Most days we now had fresh rolls and fresh milk for breakfast; I had the honour of going to buy them at half-past six at the bakery/dairy shop across the road. I am not being facetious: it was indeed a privilege and made me feel very important – and getting up at six o'clock was quite normal.

As Gerd and I went to the same school where Schalli taught, the three of us always walked together, chatting, hopping and skipping all the way. Well, Schalli didn't do a lot of hopping and skipping as she was often carrying piles of exercise books that she'd been marking the night before.

I liked the walk to school across the wide boulevard that led down to the Brandenburg Gate, past the corner cinema where Laurel and Hardy films were advertised, through the park and along the banks of a little lake (*Lietzensee*) where you could hire rowing boats in the summer and go ice skating in the winter, and eventually up the wide stone steps into the solid-looking school building. It took twenty minutes at a leisurely pace, and we always arrived in good time for the eight o'clock start.

All my teachers were Schalli's colleagues, and often her close friends. I don't remember that I found that remarkable or inhibiting in any way; it just was what it was, along with all the other necessary adjustments the move to Charlottenburg had brought with it. But

Astrid age 9, school photo

then, in those days I hadn't reached puberty and still took life as it came. Our ability to adapt is amazing; our ability to change, however, is perhaps not quite so remarkable.

Although I felt that I was only expected to be 'sweet' and 'a very good girl', now I was starting to get good marks as well. Herr Werth was an excellent teacher. He was the one who realised that I was short-sighted and needed glasses, and under his guidance I finally learned to read properly and became less confused about p's, b's, d's and g's. By the time I was ten I even read for pleasure occasionally.

I enjoyed the regular school outings with our much-loved teacher. Sometimes it was an excursion into the woods, or it could be a boat trip or a walk around the old town centre. When Herr Werth heard that many of us had never been to the cinema to see moving pictures, he took the whole class to see the Walt Disney film *Bambi*. I have no idea who paid for it; most of the parents could certainly not afford that sort of extravagance.

It was my first film ever, and I didn't know what to expect. After the initial excited babbling and restlessness, my classmates and I settled down to wide-eyed viewing, occasionally sliding forward in our seat in an unconscious attempt to edge closer to the screen. We were completely enchanted and oblivious to our surroundings.

It hadn't occurred to me to bring a handkerchief as I didn't have a cold. That was a mistake. Bambi's lovely mother gets shot and dies. All alone on his weeny, wobbly legs in the dismal, daunting woods, the cute fawn calls out to her in vain in its frightened, feeble voice. The mother died? No! Males died, men who had photos taken in uniform; grandmothers died, and grandfathers, and occasionally babies died – but a mother? I dissolved into tears.

The uncontrollable sobbing only got worse when Bambi's father, the majestic stag, appeared out of the mist and commanded, 'Come with me – my son.'

The fact that Bambi is shown at the end as a fully grown stag with babies of his own didn't comfort me. On the contrary; now cute Bambi had also disappeared from the screen. He had morphed into a grown-up within half a minute – and that was supposed to make 'it' alright?

My throat and chest were aching from suppressed howls. The mucus from my nose was joining the path of the tears and dripping liberally over my mouth and down my chin. I wiped them ineffectively with my sleeve.

As the overhead lights went on at the end of the film I was exposed, for everyone to see, with a scarlet, snot-covered, swollen-eyed face, blubbering and snivelling, and without a handkerchief to rescue me from this humiliating situation. I had to meet the scrutinising glances of Herr Werth, who was counting his flock at the exit, when all I wanted to do was wail with unconstrained grief and stirred-up emotions.

School outing 1951

That first film was a memorable outing. Although I never watched *Bambi* again – not with my children nor with my grandchildren – to this day a visit to the cinema always feels like a very special and important occasion.

The photo above was taken on one of our outings. I am on the top row, the last one on the right, the girl with the bow in her hair. Herr Werth is right at the back. The tall girl next to him is not standing on a soapbox; she is as tall as he is because she is sixteen years old. She had to go to school with us ten-year-olds because, being one of the refugees from the Ukraine,[13] she hadn't had any schooling for several years. There were often older children in lower classes for similar reasons.

---

[13] Ethnic Germans who had left their homelands in the eighteenth and nineteenth centuries and settled in territories off the north coast of the Black Sea, mostly in the territories of the southern Russian Empire (including modern-day Ukraine).

School normally finished at lunchtime, but the outings could last much longer. Some classmates, who had obligations in the afternoon like looking after their siblings, sometimes brought those siblings along, as you can see in the first row, bottom right.

Herr Werth started teaching us English in the fourth form when we were ten years old. Everybody in West Berlin and West Germany had to learn English at that age. In East Berlin, just a couple of miles down the road, children learned Russian instead. Nobody learned English in the East because, under the communist regime, that language was associated with capitalism, decadence and corruption.

The communist media ridiculed the 'bad American influence' seen in the West, generally known as the 'Coca-Cola culture': immoral dances like rock 'n' roll; depraved music like jazz; degenerate art; pornography; trashy American films; tight jeans; young girls with make-up and an altogether unhealthy, immoral lifestyle. It was true that West Germany and West Berlin started to adopt a decidedly American flavour in the wake of the American financial aid; much of the money had to be spent on American goods, boosting the post-war economy of the United States as well as the American cultural presence in West Germany.

Not everyone regarded this strong American influence as a good thing. Herr Werth definitely disapproved of some modern developments in West Berlin: 'If I ever see any of you in or near the new amusement park down the road, I shall make it my personal business to take you by the scruff of the neck and march you home.' Apparently, these new funfairs with their colourful razzmatazz were full of gangsters, prostitutes and immoral goings-on, especially at night. Herr Werth made it quite clear that he had no respect for girls wearing lipstick; a 'decent girl' showed modesty in dress and manner, and a 'decent boy' strove to become a man of honour and to behave chivalrously. My best friend Brigitte and I felt obliged to make a large detour on the way home in order to avoid passing the sinful amusement park.

When we started to learn English, Brigitte and I played at being foreigners on the way home. We would pause at a shop window and wait until we had an audience – that is, until another person also stopped. Then we would have an animated conversation in English which involved lots of gestures and facial expressions.

'Zis iss a pencil.'

'Ah yes, and zer iss a rubber.'

'Iss zis a door?'

'No, zis iss a vindow.'

Did we really think the stranger would assume that we were two little foreign girls? I think on some level we wanted to believe they would, because being a foreigner was exciting – being German was boring.

Worse still, we had subconsciously absorbed the attitude that being German wasn't desirable and somehow not attractive. That was the unspoken and undefined understanding that permeated society all around us.

*Lieber ein halber Ami als ein ganzer Nazi* (It is better to be half an American than a whole Nazi) is a commonplace saying these days. It alludes to the phenomenon that so many anglicisms have entered the German language over the recent decades that it seems as if the language has become half-American. Evidently Brigitte and I had already absorbed the nascent sentiments that would facilitate this later invasion of American words and their colonisation of the German language.

Towards the end of my primary-school years, our standard of living had much improved. My bedroom walls were adorned with pretty wallpaper, we had some basic furniture, and we shared a large orange from Florida every Saturday evening after dinner. Schalli

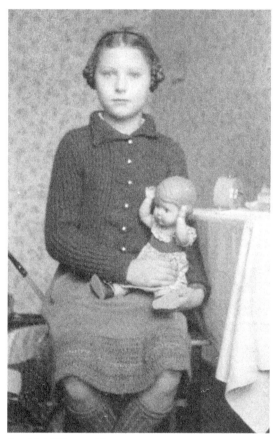

Astrid 1952, age 10

MY LIFE IN CAPITALS

always had the little irregular navel bit of the orange because she was particularly fond of that part. After carefully removing the navel and putting it on her plate, she would pass half of the orange each to Gerd and me. I really believed at the time that she was not that keen on the proper, juicy orange segments.

Gerd was already in secondary education and cycled to his school and back on a sturdy old bike we had brought back from Woltersdorf. I would need my own mode of transport soon when I started secondary school, so Schalli took me to a bicycle shop and bought a brand-new ladies' bike for me.

I was completely incredulous. I stood in the luminous shop that smelt excitingly of fresh rubber and polish and gaped in stunned silence at the rows of colourful bicycles. I was allowed to have the red one with the white tyres and glistening chrome handlebars. It had three different gears. More than sixty years later, that same bike – with replaced tyres and brakes – is still my bike when I visit Gerd in Berlin. Riding it still gives me a warm glow of pleasure as I remember the euphoric feeling, the giddy surge of elation, I experienced the day my mother bought it.

I was very much looking forward to riding my bike to the secondary school every day, wherever that might turn out to be. Brigitte and I didn't know where we would end up; we had to wait until parents and teachers had got together and decided which sort of secondary school would be appropriate for the abilities of each child, whilst taking into account the needs of their family. Many parents wanted their children to leave school as soon as possible, to get an apprenticeship and start work at fifteen. Brigitte and I had made a pact; no matter what happened, we would remain friends for the rest of our lives.

# ADOLESCENCE, SPANDAU

## 1953–1959

My mother insisted that I went to the same secondary school as my brother, although Herr Werth, my primary-school teacher who had taught me for four years and knew me well, strongly advised against a grammar school. Not that he thought I wouldn't be able to handle the academic requirements, he just thought my temperament was better suited to the more versatile, modern approach of the schools that finished at age sixteen with the O-level equivalent. But Schalli wanted both her children to finish school with the *Abitur* (A-levels). She'd had to leave school at fourteen to start earning money, and she wanted a better life for us.[14]

I liked my secondary school. It was called *Waldschule* (School in the Woods), and that was exactly what it was. The schoolrooms

---

14    Schalli did get the *Abitur* in the end, but she had to do it the hard way at evening classes whilst working full time. As it happens, that is where she met my father who was doing the same thing. I have been blessed (or cursed?) with a double inheritance of genetic programming to learn in later life.

were simple wooden huts connected by sandy paths that led through trees, shrubs and pretty little meadows with a football field right in the middle. Under the trees there were circular groups of wooden benches with attached desks; when the weather was good, lessons took place in these miniature amphitheatres.

There was a lovely feeling of freedom; what was more, my friend Brigitte was in my class and sat next to me. The class teacher rearranged the seating plan and put me next to a boy in the hope that there would be less chatter during lessons, but this ploy had limited success.

The first hut by the gate was used by the headmaster, a small man with a big stomach who looked and sounded a bit like Churchill. The first time I saw broadcasts of Churchill, I felt a cosy familiarity and found it hard to believe that he wasn't German. The headmaster would sit at his desk by the window and keep a watchful eye on the hordes of pupils arriving on their bicycles in the mornings. At quarter to eight precisely, he would get up from his seat and stand by the wide gate to catch and reprimand any latecomers. This was enough of a deterrent to make me race the last mile or so at top speed so that I often arrived bathed in sweat.

Attached to the outside of the headmaster's hut was a large thermometer, which played an important role in the life of the school. During the summer months a group of prefects gathered around it in the morning and solemnly contemplated the mercury column. If it showed twenty-five degrees Celsius or above at ten in the morning, it was customary to send everybody home because by midday it would be unbearably hot, well over thirty degrees Celsius. It was called *Hitzefrei* – 'no school because of heat'. We always carried swimsuits in our satchels, just in case. The thermometer sometimes showed impossibly high temperatures of forty degrees or more, which could only have been brought about by the subterfuge of the secret smokers (with whom the headmaster waged an endless war) using their matches and lighters.

When temperatures fell below minus ten degrees Celsius in the winter, the Churchill-lookalike headmaster didn't stand by the gate but hovered inside his hut, ready to pounce if anyone tried to sneak past because they were late. Sneaking past wasn't easy: it involved ducking below his windowsill whilst trying not to lose control of the bike you were pushing.

It was eight kilometres from our new flat in Spandau to the *Waldschule,* and the ride took me about thirty minutes. In the winter there was usually snow, which prolonged the journey substantially particularly as the school lay atop a slight hill. One of the worst pains I have ever experienced was the sensation of blood returning to hands that had held metal handlebars for forty minutes in sub-zero temperatures without gloves. I did have some gloves, of course, but as a teenager I tended to lose or misplace things like gloves, scarves, books, homework or keys on a regular basis.

The headmaster taught history, but I never had lessons with him. My history teacher was special: he had a false leg! During the tests that we had to sit every two or three weeks, he would take off his wooden leg, put it on the desk in front of him, and rub his aching stump through his trousers. If he suspected anyone of cheating, or if he felt particularly bored, he would take the leg in both hands and prod us with it or bang it on our desk whilst hopping on the other. Or he would leave the wooden leg on his desk and hop around the room on his good leg, singing an aria from a famous German opera under his breath, 'Oh, I am clever and wise, and I will not be cheated,'[15] whilst we were trying to scribble the answers to his questions.

---

[15]   *Zar und Zimmermann* by Albert Lortzing (1801–1851). Aria '*Oh, ich bin klug und weise, und mich betrügt man nicht*'.

His constant talking and singing about stopping us from cheating started to feel like a challenge to me, a provocation. I began to write some key facts with biro on my thighs where the skin was covered by my knee-length skirt, a strategy that was not exactly conducive to learning. I was never caught looking at the notes, but I naturally had to share the information with Christian, the boy sitting next to me, who could see what was going on.

The large wall map our history teacher used showed the borders of Germany from the 1870s, making it look almost twice as big as it actually had been since 1945. It looked as if Berlin was smack in the middle of a large country. The territories east of the Oder-Neisse line,[16] which were given to Poland and Russia after the end of the war, were marked in pencil as 'temporarily under Polish/Russian administration'. I guess up-to-date school maps hadn't yet been printed. My generation probably grew up with quite misleading ideas about Germany's borders; I definitely did.

The history lessons never went further than Bismarck and the foundation of the German Reich in 1871. At that point, the curriculum started again with Ancient Greece and the Roman Empire. We weren't taught anything about the First or Second World Wars. The term 'Jews' was never mentioned. Later I realised that most of our teachers must have been participants in the war which had, after all, only finished eight years previously. The war was never referred to explicitly and seemed as irrelevant and distant to me as the Thirty Years' War of the seventeenth century.

Thirty years later, the opposite was the case: the next generation indulged in never-ending contemplation about the Second World War. The role the Nazis played and the guilt or innocence of the Germans

---

[16]   The rivers Oder and Neisse, not far from Berlin, have marked the border to Poland since 1945.

was analysed incessantly in schoolrooms by people who had no personal experience whatsoever of that epoch.

I neither liked nor particularly disliked history. My best, and therefore favourite, subjects (or my favourite, and therefore best, subjects) were music, sport, mathematics, Latin and biology. My least favourite subjects were geography, English, French and chemistry. During these, I joined the disruptive elements in the class and showed off to the naughty boys by being even more outrageous than they were.

I played football and other ball games with them during break; in class I was quite skilful at tossing balls, rubbers and copybooks around, or throwing objects like banana skins or snowballs at the teacher the moment he turned his back. When I was fifteen, Schalli received a letter of complaint from the school about my behaviour and increasingly bad results in some subjects.

The key expressions in my diary at the time were *Why? What the hell for? What is the purpose of life and everything?*[17] But above all, *Boring ... longing for ... waiting.* I used to stand by my window and watch the teenage twins in the block of flats opposite our home, who were about my age, flirting with boys by their front door. Boys on mopeds with Elvis hairstyles came from far and wide to be teased by them and taunted by their red-painted lips, waspy waists, swinging skirts and tantalising giggles. I felt painfully envious and isolated – life was passing me by.

Brigitte came to visit me sometimes and we would try out some lipstick and a cigarette or starch our petticoats in sugar-water in the bath, but that was just 'practising for the real thing'. We pranced around in front of a mirror trying to blow smoke rings, and I would

---

[17] I have learnt since then that the answer to that vital question is of course 42. (See *Hitchhiker's Guide to the Galaxy*)

MY LIFE IN CAPITALS

pluck Brigitte's eyebrows. I didn't have any eyebrows to speak of and pencilled mine in instead – with a normal pencil.

Schalli started to disapprove of my friendship with Brigitte; she was suddenly considered a bad influence and not welcome in our home. That threw me completely; my loyalties were divided and for a while I didn't know what to do. The balance was eventually tipped in favour of Brigitte, and I started going to her place instead, more or less secretly, and we remain friends to this day.[18] The short entry from my diary reads: *I wish to note here for the future that I must do my best never to voice criticism about the friends of my children. Schalli spoke badly about Brigitte, and that has annoyed me intensely.* I hope I managed to keep to this resolution.

For a whole year I went with Gerd to an old-fashioned dance school where we learnt to do the foxtrot, waltz and tango, but I wanted to do the rock 'n' roll and jive to the music of Elvis Presley. Doing the antiquated dances was about as exciting as slurping lukewarm soup when you wanted to chew on a juicy hot steak. My dance partners were usually half a head smaller than me and tended to be spotty sixteen-year-olds in pretentious suits.

The only amusing bit was when the dance instructor would shout '*Beckenkontakt*' (pelvic contact) in the voice of a sergeant major, hoping in vain for dance partners to reduce the huge gap between their bodies. *Beckenkontakt* was especially important for the tango. The instructors would demonstrate the tight fit of their bodies and their intertwined thighs without much success; the girls giggled, and the boys went red in the face. The moment the tango music started up, lots of boys would excuse themselves and dash to the toilet. When I see *Strictly Come Dancing* on the television these days, I always

---

[18]    I am godmother to her second child, who is grown-up now and lives in Ethiopia.

Astrid and Gerd 1957

notice the excellent *Beckenkontakt* of the participants. As they say, 'No knowledge is ever wasted.'

Although there were no nightclubs where teenagers could rock 'n' roll to their hearts' content, there were plenty of cultural venues to go to. A visit to the theatre, concert or opera cost fifty *Pfennige* as part of a special programme for schoolchildren. That was about the same as the cost of the underground there and back, which was also subsidised. It was very cheap for adults too, thanks to generous Western backing.

From the mid-1950s onwards West Berlin was artificially propped up as a showcase, with special support for commerce and industry and all sorts of price reductions, like cheap bread and milk. There was even exemption from military service for all young men – as long as they remained in West Berlin. This was to stop West Berlin becoming a city of old people; not having to spend eighteen months doing military service encouraged many young people to stay in the sealed-off town.

Several times a month my schoolfriends and I, or Gerd and I, would go to a play, concert, opera or art exhibition. The most famous musicians, actors and shows were enticed to West Berlin, but they were largely wasted on me. It all seemed awfully straitlaced and dated. I didn't understand the classical plays; the ballets were strangely beautiful but boring; I liked the concerts, but I couldn't keep my eyes open; the operas, with the large-bosomed matrons bursting your eardrums and playing young maidens in love dying on the stage for hours on end, seemed embarrassingly ridiculous.

I heard Wagner's *Ring Cycle*, all fifteen hours of it, in one week. According to our music teacher, it was a special production that could not be missed. I am sure it was an unusual 'once in a lifetime' production and I have not forgotten it, not because of the music or artistic value but because each of the four operas had two or even three intermissions when I could drink Coca-Cola, perched on a bar stool in the plush saloon bar.

Getting home after a performance was no problem. The underground, the buses and the *S-Bahn* (city train) ran all night, just not as often as during the daytime. Schalli's strict curfew regulation, 'home at nine o'clock promptly, no matter what', was lifted for these cultural excursions.

She had to wait up for me because, having lost my first one, I was no longer entrusted with a house key. She would greet me with the familiar, weary sounding, 'Have you wiped your feet? Go and wash your hands. Don't forget to turn off the light.' This was often followed by, 'Your room is a disgrace – it looks as if the devil has torn himself to shreds in there. I don't understand how you can live like that.'

She was right. Getting ready to go out took a long time and involved trying on every single item of clothing and discarding unsuitable pieces onto the floor with increasing haste and carelessness.

I felt that my mother was saying the same things over and over again, using the same phrases in the same tone of voice, making the same criticisms. Instead of changing my ways, my feelings towards her hardened and I developed a way of staring into the middle distance behind her head. It drove her mad.

'Don't do that. You are looking at me in that weird way again.'

My predictable answer was, 'What do you mean? I am listening to you.' But that was about as far as my rebelliousness went.

I never dared to start a full-blown argument or blatantly test Schalli's authority, although she didn't hit us any longer. When Gerd was about fifteen, she was about to smack him for one reason or another, when she stopped with her arm raised in mid-air and started laughing. 'I actually have to reach up to slap you. That's it, you are taller than me now and I can't do this anymore.'

In order to avoid unnecessary confrontation, my mother developed a clever strategy. When she got home after a heavy day's teaching, she shouted, 'I am not home yet,' whilst taking off her coat and disappearing into her room. For about twenty to thirty minutes there was dead silence and then she would surface with a friendly, 'Hello, I'm home!' and go into the kitchen to fix our dinner. This was often followed by the three of us sitting in Schalli's room listening to the radio whilst cuddling or knitting or playing cards.

One day, she came out of her room with a letter in her hand. 'Your headmaster has written to say you have to repeat the last school year.'

This was horrifying! I knew my marks in chemistry and geography were bad, but I had hoped that the good marks in some other subjects would counterbalance them. I somehow thought *sitzenbleiben* (being put back a year and having to repeat the whole year's curriculum) was something that only happened to 'thickos', that it could never happen to me.

Schalli was unusually calm and composed. 'What are we going to do about this?'

The answer was clear to me. I defiantly declared that, as I was fifteen, I was old enough to leave school. I would leave school right now and start work.

That turned out to be an unacceptable option. 'You can't go through life without a final school certificate!'

We compromised; as I couldn't face the idea of four more years of school (with children who had been a year below me), it was decided that I would only repeat Year Ten, this time pass all thirteen subjects and leave with a school certificate equivalent to O-levels.

There followed a year of 'stiff upper lip', of not showing my deep humiliation and shame. *I won't give them the satisfaction*, it says in my diary, though it is not clear who 'they' were, nor why 'they' would be pleased about my failure. Our relatives and the people in the house weren't informed about this social disgrace.

At school there was no longer any throwing of banana skins or jumping out of windows instead of using the door. I was well-behaved, but I felt isolated. Brigitte had passed the Year Ten tests and left school to take a secretarial training course. That was rather pleasing, insofar as we were now 'outcasts' together and not part of the body of respectable Year Eleven pupils striving towards their A-Levels.

Christian remained friends with me. He missed the secret information my thighs had provided for him during examinations. We used to share half a cigarette behind the headmaster's hut and discuss the woes of the world. 'My problem is that I am a girl in a boy's body,' he said, according to my diary. 'And your problem is exactly the same – just the other way around. You think and act like a boy.'[19] I was flattered.

---

[19]  I was surprised to find this diary entry, because somehow I thought all the intricate gender problems upsetting the present young generation were a new development.

A year later, at sixteen, I obtained a reasonable end-of-year certificate. I had managed to pass chemistry and geography, though my marks hadn't improved in the other eleven subjects: they were either the same as the previous year or had actually gone down. Repetition does not always produce better results; it doesn't stimulate interest and therefore doesn't increase competence in a subject. But I passed and could leave school, as Schalli had promised.

As I didn't seem to have any plans and answered any queries about my future with a sulky, 'Whatever!' Schalli decided I should start work in the pharmaceutical industry. Maybe she thought the appointment was a sort of apprenticeship and my Latin would come in useful. Or, my teenage brain wondered, was her intention to punish me and teach me a lesson?

The job was repetitive; all I did month after month was fill shelves with pharmaceutical products in a wholesale warehouse. It was a large cellar lit by fierce fluorescent lights. I was supposed to assist a withered, little old man in charge of shelves A–F.

The women in the offices upstairs received orders from various chemists and hospitals and sent the order forms down to us through pneumatic tubes. The cylindrical containers arrived at our station with a satisfying *pffffTHUNK*! created by the compressed air. That was the best bit. But putting the requested items from the shelves into a basket was beyond me because there were hundreds of drugs and medicines, and they were not sorted alphabetically by their product name but by the manufacturer. An order might say '20 x Aspirin 500 tablets @ 80mg' and you had to know that they were on the shelf under B for Bayer.

We worked a normal forty-eight-hour week: eight hours a day, Monday to Saturday, with Sunday off. I now had the social independence and autonomy I had sought, but I really didn't like the job. There were no other youngsters, and the women with whom I had lunch in the canteen seemed worse than children to me; they were forever gossiping, complaining, fighting and forming groups of 'us' and 'them'. In the end I used to dash out and sit on a park bench by myself for twenty minutes, eating a sandwich and soaking up the sun and fresh air.

I had to get up even earlier than I had done for school to catch the six-thirty train into town. On the way home I regularly fell asleep in the *S-Bahn,* which was a bit of a problem because Spandau lay at the edge of West Berlin and our station was the last one in the West. I relied on the warning announcements over the Tannoy system or the other passengers to wake me up.

The border was only two miles away from our home so whenever you left the house there was only one direction to go, towards the city centre. We were totally cut off from the surrounding countryside, which produced a muted but persistent feeling of confinement.

On New Year's Eve, the island existence of West Berlin became very apparent. Every family, every household was by the radio listening to the speech of West Berlin's Mayor, ready with their subsidised rockets, screamers and bangers. At the last stroke of the midnight hour, the city seemed to explode as a fury of light and noise erupted in the skies (and in the hallways) with deafening bangs and crackles. Cats vanished under the beds and dogs were fitted with earmuffs for the next hour or so. The air was flooded with the smell of gunpowder. All cars had disappeared from the streets and even the taxi drivers refused to be on the road. Extravagant public firework displays across the city added to the impression of Armageddon.

Schalli didn't really like it – I think it reminded her too much of more serious explosions. We stood on our balcony waving our modest sparklers, shouting 'Happy New Year' to the other residents and enjoying the spectacle. We had a good view from our fourth-floor flat. In one direction, we could see hundreds of rockets shooting into the sky, fountains of fiery sparks and bright flowers at a great height bursting into breath-taking light. Catherine wheels with vivid colours illuminated the night-sky and everything was accompanied by the deafening sounds of *whoosh, bang, whistle* and *whizz*.

Looking in the other direction, the direction of the nearby border, there was absolute silence and darkness. Our cleaning lady from East Berlin said that, observing the spectacle from the outside, it looked like the glowing plume over Hiroshima, this island of western values exploding, surrounded by the quiet red sea of communism.

At some time during my unhappy working life, Schalli took me for an aptitude test to see if we could do better than the pharmaceutical firm. Afterwards we were handed a list of suggested occupations suitable for a young lady with my capabilities: shop assistant, hairdresser, nurse, working with technical drawings.

Amongst them was something I had never heard of before. It was explained to us that this was a very new profession called *Krankengymnastik* meaning 'gymnastics for sick people'. I thought that might be a possibility because I was rather keen on gymnastics and working with a team to help sick people to get better sounded a lot more fun than stocking shelves in a cellar. In England, this profession is called physiotherapy – but I think that term would have put me off with its learned-sounding Greek origins.

We went to look at the training establishment and I was thrilled! It was like a school for young adults, with a wide-ranging timetable of practical sessions and lectures in rooms bathed in sunlight. Animated-looking young women in black leotards ran past us on their way to do gymnastics.

The fact that you couldn't start the training until you were eighteen and had to do six months unpaid work experience in a hospital beforehand, was no problem. I immediately left the warehouse and worked for six months as an auxiliary nurse on a children's ward. I loved it. My previous lethargy disappeared, and I no longer felt at all tired. On free evenings, when I was not on duty, I earned some money working in the NAAFI[20] in Spandau.

Spandau was part of the British sector. Smuts Barracks, where the British infantry battalion was stationed, was only a ten-minute walk from home and they always needed young *Fräuleins* to help out in the canteen.

I felt it was quite an adventure because I had to walk past Spandau Prison where Rudolf Hess and some other war criminals were incarcerated.[21] Every month there were different guards, alternating between British, French, American and Russian. I would walk bravely past these fierce-looking sentries and turn into the British garrison next door.

Luckily, the staff in the officers' mess where I worked were all German. My English was still rudimentary, and I really couldn't understand a word the Scottish soldiers who were stationed there were saying. I worked behind the bar and somehow managed to take their orders, which fortunately consisted mainly of Oxo cubes dissolved in hot water. They didn't have much money to spend.

The British soldiers always stood out like sore thumbs when they ventured forth into town wearing their civilian clothes. Apparently, they didn't even own proper coats and hats to wear in winter!

'Look, here comes one of those poor English lads,' people used to say. 'The little houses in their family quarters don't even have lace curtains at the windows!' The first thing any self-respecting German housewife would do when moving into a new place would be to put up lace curtains. It never occurred to us that the English housewives

---

20    NAAFI: The Navy, Army and Air Force Institute

21    After the death of Rudolf Hess in 1987, Spandau Prison was demolished to prevent it from becoming a neo-Nazi shrine. A shopping centre for the British forces was erected on the site, which was nicknamed Hessco's.

might have had 'naked windows' by choice.

Although my English was very poor, I had no trouble understanding Johnnie when he asked if he could walk me home one day. The whole mess erupted in good-natured heckling as we left because he was one of the young, shy officers. We didn't have much to say to each other, but it felt nice walking next to him.

At the entrance to my block of flats he kissed me briefly on the lips and left. Each evening the kiss grew a little longer, until that awful night when we stood entwined in the dark just inside the door and heard footsteps coming to a halt outside. The key turned, a woman entered and put on the stair lights. It was Schalli, whom I had presumed safely tucked up in bed.

She glared at us, almost speechless. All she managed to splutter was 'Upstairs!' How could I? On the public stairway! With a soldier! Like a common tart! Did the commanding officer of the garrison know that I was underage? She would put an end to this! And she did. She went to the barracks and terminated my employment, and I had to promise never to go anywhere near the place again.

That was roughly when the obligatory placement at the hospital came to an end. I was seventeen years old and there were still more than six months before I could start the physiotherapy training. The urge to get away, to see the world and have an adventure, was overwhelming.

Schalli refused to support such an adventure in any way. When I stubbornly declared, I would go to England without her help, she pointed out that you had to be eighteen and needed a work permit to live in another European country. I made an impulsive decision: I would go and see Auntie Helga, who now lived in Brussels with her husband and three small children. Schalli reluctantly gave her permission and paid the train fare, expecting me to come home a few weeks later.

# LEAVING BERLIN

## 1959

The train journey from Berlin to Brussels took about nine hours, including border controls and a change of trains in Aachen. I had visited Auntie Helga twice before by myself and felt quite relaxed and confident. I was particularly lucky this time; not only did I find a seat by the window, but I managed to put my little suitcase on the overhead storage shelf before attracting the attention of any male passengers. They would invariably step up behind you and help lift your luggage, more often than not using the opportunity to brush a little too close for comfort.

During the first three hours, all doors and windows were locked whilst travelling from West Berlin through the Russian zone towards West Germany. This was not too much of a problem because it was January; nonetheless, in order to prevent the little compartment, with seating for eight people, from getting too stuffy, the sliding door to the side corridor was left open. As a result, the cigarette smoke from people standing in the narrow corridor wafted into the cubicle, mingling strangely with the existing odours of musty upholstery, cheese sandwiches and damp coats. Everybody knew that we were not locked in to stop us leaving the train – nobody in their right mind would want to escape into the East.

'Heaven knows what they think they're achieving by locking us in like this,' the woman sitting opposite me volunteered, addressing herself to nobody in particular.

Her remark opened the floodgates. 'They're not locking us in, my dear lady – they're locking their own citizens out, making sure no one can board the train to get to the West,' a passenger replied.

A third joined in. 'No, they're just playing the old power game. They're only trying to intimidate us and remind us that the whole of West Berlin is at their mercy.'

'Well, they're succeeding with me. I do feel claustrophobic and trapped, all locked in like this,' a little old lady from the seat by the door declared, whilst straightening her smart travel hat on her tightly permed hair. 'I used to throw food parcels to my relatives from the train windows,' she continued. 'Great shame we can't do that anymore because sending the stuff by post is really daunting, having to fill in all those forms and declarations – and nine times out of ten the parcel arrives ripped open with the best bits missing.'

'True, true. Those commies who are "more equal than others" must have quite a nice little stash of coffee, chocolate and leather boots by now,' chuckled the man sitting next to me.

I sat by the window pretending to be fascinated by the landscape as it rushed by. In truth, I was avoiding talking to total strangers and was taking the opportunity to consider my situation. One thing was for sure: despite Schalli expecting me home in two or three weeks' time, I would not go back to Berlin until the late autumn when the physiotherapy course was due to start. Rather than entering into negotiations with her and risking a ban, which I would not feel able to disobey, I would present my mother with a *fait accompli*.

I was convinced that the ensuing months presented a unique opportunity, the like of which would never occur in my life again – and I was probably right. There I was, young, strong, healthy and absolutely free, with no ties whatsoever, yet there seemed nowhere suitable to 'start living'. My diary at this time is full of pseudo-philosophical observations and frustrated, glib statements: *You seem to get everything you want in life – but just not always when it is convenient and at a time you want it,* and *Youth is wasted on the young.*

I stared absent-mindedly out of the window and contemplated my meagre options. The British Ministry of Labour had refused to give me a labour permit because I was under eighteen, besides which they asked for proof that you had a job to go to. Without a labour permit, it wasn't possible to enter Great Britain for more than a few weeks. Working somewhere in West Germany would be utterly pedestrian – I might as well have stayed in Berlin and worked in the pharmaceutical warehouse. France and Belgium were just as difficult as far as labour permits were concerned, and out of the question anyway because my French was even worse than my English.

I didn't even consider America; a week on a boat suffering from seasickness was more than off-putting. There were some transatlantic flights, but it was not until the early 1970s that travel by aeroplane became a reality for the masses. And anyway, how would I get there without money, not to mention the absence of a visa? All my hopes were pinned on Auntie Helga's ingenuity.

I felt positive about my immediate future. My life was constantly improving; better food; better living conditions; better clothes; ownership of a bicycle; smaller classes at school, and an interesting profession to look forward to – the complete list would be very long. Things that had been deemed impossible had become possible overnight. I had been taught, for instance, that the dark side of the moon, the side eternally facing away from earth, would remain a mystery forever. But my teachers were wrong, because here were people on my train showing each other pictures in ordinary newspapers of the very same 'never-attainable sight', captured and photographed by none other than a Russian lunar probe called Sputnik. A lot of tutting and sucking of teeth went on in the train compartment.

'They can't provide decent nourishment for their citizens, but they've got the technology to be the first humans to look at the dark side of the moon.'

'The Americans won't like that. This is bad news for us,' was the general consensus of my travelling companions, because West Berlin was considered the most feasible place for any violent collision of the giants.

'And this communist chap Fidel Castro is in charge in Cuba now. They'll like that even less – a communist country on their doorstep.'

Apparently, with Cuba only ninety miles away from Florida, the Americans would feel threatened.[22] Yet none of this worried me. We hardly ever talked about politics and current world affairs at home or at school. We didn't own a TV set and I never listened to boring, adult newscasts on my little radio. My cousins living in the eastern zone listened to Russian folk songs and stirring Russian ballads, while my radio was permanently tuned into Radio Luxembourg or the AFN, both of which played non-stop American pop music.[23] Politics, and the worries connected with them, were somehow not part of my life. I felt invincible.

When the conversation in the train compartment started getting more intense, I decided it was time to stand outside in the corridor

---

[22]    As it turned out they did feel threatened, so much so that by the time I celebrated my twenty-first birthday four years later the situation had accelerated to the point of an imminent nuclear war.

[23]    I only learned recently that the youngsters in the UK listened to the very same radio stations at the time!

The *Atomium* in Brussels

and puff vigorously on a cigarette, pretending to inhale deeply. But no young rock star came sidling down the aisle to befriend the young woman with the despicable smoking addiction. Instead, I could still hear them talking. Now it was about the Dalai Lama and how thousands of Tibetans were fleeing to India, and how nobody knew what was going on in China as Mao had cut all ties with the outside world and had closed his borders completely.

When the unusually shaped Atomium building finally came into sight, everyone's mood seemed to lift. I had visited the Brussels World's Fair (also known as Expo 58)[24] with Auntie Helga the previous year and had wandered through this 'atom-shaped' building in absolute awe. The Atomium had been at the entrance to the exhibition and its main attraction, just like the Eiffel Tower had been built as the main attraction for the Paris World's Fair in 1889. For me, the Atomium

---

[24]   The Brussels World's Fair saw more than 41,000,000 visitors.

symbolised – and still symbolises – modernity and hope, all that is uplifting, inspirational and positive in human endeavour.

The moment I stepped from the train, I knew I was in a different country. The plants, the wind and the sky were the same, but the way people moved and dressed, and above all the foreign voices, seemed excitingly different. From a distance, German conversation always sounds to me as if people are arguing or are at least in a huff. French sounds more like a benevolent dragon cooing to its brood, words emanating like steam from deep in the throat via puckered lips at express velocity.

The first time I heard my teacher speak French, I assumed she had a throat infection and a blocked nose; I was amazed that the congestion miraculously disappeared when she went back to German. French sounds fascinatingly elegant and superior but trying to imitate that 'snotty-nosed' intonation is far too embarrassing and therefore out of the question. No wonder nobody in Brussels understood the few words I said.

Fortunately, I had come equipped with some Belgian francs. I knew which tram to take, how to get the ticket from a machine and where to get off, so no talking was necessary. Walking past the strange-smelling shops with *Boucherie* and *Boulangerie* written above the slightly dirty shop windows made me feel like an intruder, a spy, an explorer, all rolled into one. There was a strong notion of 'not belonging', which gave rise to a wonderful feeling of freedom.

When people ask me why I subsequently came to England, I like to point with a melodramatic gesture to my heart and say, 'It was love!'[25] But that is not true; I hadn't even met my future husband at that point. I came to England in search of that feeling of 'lightness of life' which

---

[25] Unless I do the 'because biting your nails is not an unforgivable sin in England'.

I experienced in Brussels whilst walking towards my aunt's block of flats. Or is that also not true? Perhaps the real origins for our actions and emotions are so complex and hidden in the subconscious that they are beyond any meaningful analysis. If that is the case, it may be wiser to adopt the attitude of the student in Alan Bennett's *The History Boys* who doesn't query the whys and wherefores, but shrugs his shoulders and says, 'History is just one bloody thing after another.'

When I knocked at the familiar door of the first-floor flat, nothing happened for a while. Perhaps they hadn't received the letter I had sent, or perhaps they had forgotten that I was coming today. Then I heard some scuffling, scraping sounds from the other side of the door. After a while someone repeatedly tried to turn the latch, and eventually the door opened an inch or two.

As nothing else happened I gently tried to push the door open and called out to Auntie Helga, but something was behind it, blocking it. I managed to put my head through the gap and saw what the problem was: Karin, aged three, was climbing off the stool she had pushed against the door in order to reach the latch. My godchild Hannes, aged one and a half, was toddling toward me, completely naked, grinning widely, dragging a heavily-soiled towelling nappy behind him with one foot. His clothes, smeared with his excrement, were strewn all over the floor. Karin had obviously been trying to clean him up.

I managed to say something like, 'Is Mummy home?', whereupon Karin put a finger to her lips and whispered, 'She is in bed.'

In the front room, Friedhelm, aged five, was sitting on the floor surrounded by a barrage of toys, concentrating on an important piece of construction work. The kitchen looked as if Karin had been active there too, with flour and sugar strewn over the table and floor mixed with the odd cereal packet and puddle of milk.

Auntie Helga, aged forty-two, lay in bed with her eyes closed. I thought for a moment that she was dead and gingerly touched her arm.

She opened her eyes, smiled and said, 'Ah, there you are. I have been waiting for you. Be a dear and hand me the tray of tablets from the top shelf. And fetch me a glass of water, please.'

I knew she'd had rheumatoid arthritis since childhood but didn't realise it occasionally rendered her completely immobile. She understood that the strong cortisone tablets and injections would kill her prematurely, but she used to say cheerfully, 'None of us get out of this alive, and I rather have quality than quantity anytime. Besides, the children need me to be fit.'

She must have taken one of her magic 'emergency remedies' because within minutes she was out of bed and dressed. The children were hugged and fed, and the flat was tidied in a joyful whirlwind flurry. We dressed the children and went down to the local shop, where everybody – shop assistants and customers alike – seemed to know and like Auntie Helga, even though she was German.

I hardly noticed her swollen, disfigured joints – not when I used to sit on her lap in Woltersdorf, nor now. All I was aware of was her warmth and cheerfulness and an atmosphere of fun wherever she went. No wonder Schalli was good friends with her and always spoke highly of her sister-in-law in those days.

By the time Auntie Helga's husband came home, all the floors, tables, faces and bums had been thoroughly wiped and dinner was on the table. Uncle Hans worked in the German Embassy and had his finger on the pulse of social developments. When he heard about my dilemma, he had a bright idea: why not try and become a 'house-daughter' to a family in England? This was a new way for youngsters to experience foreign cultures and was called 'being an au pair'.[26] The same evening, he helped me to write to an au pair agency in London

---

[26] The European Agreement on Au Pair Placement was only signed in 1969 and came into force in 1971.

and asked for any replies to be sent to the address in Brussels.

And then we waited. A profound melancholic longing took hold of me; I felt an irrational sense of yearning – for what exactly, I didn't know. I clearly remember standing on the beach at Ostend during one of our outings, thrusting my face into the chilly gusts of wind coming from the sea, imagining the oh-so-close English shoreline just below the horizon, and willing a reaction from beyond my reach. Whilst I was building sandcastles in the sky, my little cousins, snugly kitted out with woolly hats, wellington boots and waterproof trousers, were constructing real sandcastles at my feet.[27]

A letter from England arrived within a week, though it felt like a month. There were no pictures, just pages and pages of text in English. Uncle Hans helped me unravel the meaning of it all, assisted with filling in the forms, and then left me to choose from two dozen or so families who wanted au pairs.

What choices! Five children, all under the age of seven, somewhere on a remote farm need help as their mother is expecting another baby – I don't think so! Out came Auntie Helga's old school atlas. It soon became clear that all the submissions from Hertford, Hereford, and Hampshire were far too mundane and likely to prove hard work for a city girl like me, even though I knew that 'hurricanes hardly ever happened there'. Our English teacher had used quotations from Bernard Shaw for our pronunciation exercises.[28] But now that I could see where these places were situated – hurricanes or not – there was only one location for me: London, or the London suburbs.

---

[27] How would I have reacted if someone had told me that Helga's little daughter, Karin, playing at my feet, was already carrying the very egg in her ovaries from which her daughter would be created, who would turn up on my doorstep in England as an adult fifty years later?

[28] Not realising that *My Fair Lady* is based on Shaw's *Pygmalion*, I was quite surprised to hear Audrey Hepburn 'steal' several of those axioms when I saw the film a few years later.

By far the easiest-sounding family lived in Surbiton, outside Kingston. They had one eight-year-old girl, who would be at school most of the time, and a black miniature poodle to take care of. There was no heavy housework as they had a cleaning lady twice a week. The au pair would have a morning off during the week to go to English lessons, either Saturday or Sunday off as well, and pocket money of thirty shillings per week.

I wrote to Mrs Dixon-Child and was surprised to receive a telegram the very next morning asking when I could start. A couple of telegrams later, all was arranged. Mrs Dixon-Child would meet me at Victoria Station; for identification, we were both to hold the last telegram in our hand. I would have preferred something more theatrical, like a white carnation in a buttonhole, but there was no time to worry about the finer details.

Uncle Hans paid for the journey, and Auntie Helga gave me a little travelling money from her secret stash. I was under no circumstances to let Uncle Hans know about this, as he was unaware that she had some money of her own that she had saved for emergencies from the housekeeping he gave her once a week.

Auntie Helga must have thought that Schalli was aware of my plans and approved of them. The subject of how my mother felt about all this was never raised, and I certainly wasn't going to bring it up. I didn't lie; I just wasn't asked the right questions.

When Schalli found out later that Auntie Helga and Uncle Hans had not only financed my escapade but had organised and encouraged it, she was outraged. She never forgave Auntie Helga. Assisting a teenager, who was still a minor, to go to a foreign country without consulting the mother was to Schalli a deceitful, unforgivable stab in the back.

The ferry Auntie Helga had booked ran from Ostend to Dover. I had never been on a large ship, let alone one that carried cars on its lower deck. The ferry seemed huge, with wide staircases, a restaurant, a duty-free shop and bunk beds below. Beds were surely not necessary whilst crossing the Channel? I knew it was a lot wider than our canal back in Berlin. You couldn't even see the other side in the poor weather conditions on the day I travelled, but it surely couldn't take more than twenty minutes or so to cross?

Had I taken the trouble to look at a map, I would have realised that Ostend to Dover is not a route that crosses the narrowest part of the Channel but is, in fact, a journey that takes several hours. But in those days, I seemed to live by the motto: 'I know best and would rather get things wrong ten times than ask once for accurate information.'

I thought I had better hurry if I wanted to buy some duty-free chocolates. I had to wait a while because the shop only opened when the ferry entered neutral waters that belonged to neither Belgium nor to England; only then could the tax-free status come into force. There were regulations on the wall about how much alcohol, cigarettes and chocolate a person was allowed to purchase and what the items cost in various European currencies.

Standing below deck in the duty-free queue didn't seem to agree with my stomach. By the time I had made my purchase of Toblerone, I felt quite queasy and decided to make use of one of those bunk beds after all, just for a few minutes because surely we had almost reached the other side of the Channel.

I must have fallen asleep because I woke up with a start, feeling very nauseous and knowing that I had to throw up. After hanging with my head over a disgusting toilet and vomiting until there seemed nothing left in my stomach, I thought I had better go and see what the English coast looked like.

The fresh air on deck gave temporary relief to my seasickness – but there was no coastline anywhere, neither behind us nor in front of us. We were on an ocean. I was on the wrong ferry, going God knows where. I didn't possess a watch and had lost all sense of time. If Auntie Helga had given me a timetable of my journey, I had either lost it or didn't consider looking at it. Feeling retchingly wretched, I hung over the railing 'feeding the fish' occasionally, thinking that this would never end.

Hours later, like a phoenix rising, a long bright structure appeared out of the mist – the famous white cliffs of Dover. As we got closer, their dramatic grandeur and imposing beauty hit me so forcefully that I forgot all about my seasickness. I gaped in awe at the immense height of this gigantic slice of chalk. It looked as if a giant monster had torn a mountain in half, thrown one half into the sea and left the sheer drop of the remaining structure standing in embarrassing nakedness with its private inside layers in full view. How could this huge white mass be made of nothing but microscopic, calcified creatures that had lived millions of years ago at the bottom of the sea? And how could the bottom of the sea end up high in the sky, providing the very foundation for terrestrial life?

At the top of the chalk, I made out a sliver of green and some tiny rooftops. A feeling of euphoria swept over me. This was it! This was England! I had arrived!

# AN AU PAIR IN ENGLAND

## 1959

The quaint British steam engine huffed and puffed towards London, occasionally sounding a cheerful whistle. I knew I had to travel to the end of the line, so I sat gazing calmly at the pretty stone-arched bridges, gently sloping hills and unfinished-looking rows of terraced houses. 'The English probably only render the front of their houses,' I thought, 'and leave the back in crude bricks.' It wasn't until much later that I realised that this dirty-red-brick look wasn't 'work in progress' or due to war, but the finished surface.

The windowpanes were flush with the outside walls, making the terraced houses look like factories. If it hadn't been for women hanging laundry on long washing lines in their backyards, I would have thought these were indeed some sort of warehouses. Being used to living in flats with lots of staircases, I fondly imagined myself living an eccentric life in one of these little houses for the next few months, helping to bring in the washing and waving to the picturesque steam locomotives.

Victoria Station turned out to be a huge complex of criss-crossing rails and countless platforms under high, dome-shaped, dirty glass ceilings. The locomotive gave one last sigh, shuddered and expired. Doors were flung open, and crowds of passengers swarmed onto the platform with their heavy suitcases, rucksacks and bags, shoving and pushing in all directions.

I suddenly felt apprehensive. I took my time and only got off the train after the first mad rush had eased a little, so that I would have a chance to spot a woman waving a telegram. Ten minutes later, I still hadn't caught sight of anyone even vaguely matching that description.

I slowly made my way along the platform, nervously displaying my telegram, and stopped by the ticket inspector who guarded the exit. After I had shown him my ticket, he said something to me that I didn't understand and then waved me through the gate.

I came to a halt a few yards away from the gate and decided to 'take root'. Schalli had always said that if you are lost or don't know where to go, simply stop and stay where you are until something happens. But nothing happened.

As my fellow travellers dispersed, the huge station appeared increasingly quiet and empty. The ticket inspector sat on a footstool by his gate, looking in my direction every now and then. I stood next to my little suitcase, telegram in hand, trying not to look at him. There were no more people on the platform; surely he should have closed the gate by now?

We both heard it at the same time and turned our heads in the direction of the approaching sound: hard heels clicking very quickly and purposefully on the tiled floor. A tall, platinum-blonde woman with bright red lips in a swaying fur coat and high stiletto heels dashed towards me – not waving a telegram, but a sandwich.

Whilst talking at a furious speed, occasionally punctuating the torrent with extraordinary high-pitched squeaks, she grabbed me with her long fingers and painted nails, sat me down on a large semi-circular wrought iron bench, pushed the limp sandwich into my hands and disappeared again, still talking about heaven knows what. When I saw the animated Disney film *One Hundred and One Dalmatians* two years later, Cruella De Vil reminded me straight away of Mrs Dixon-Child. But at least we had found each other, and she knew where I was.

Bewildered, I sat there and looked at the sandwich: cheese and tomato. What sort of a combination was that, for heaven's sake? Cheese and fruit. It seemed totally incompatible. I ate it, of course, because I was hungry and because I was used to eating whatever was put in front of me. Later in life, I considered combinations like cheese with pineapple cubes on cocktail sticks to be the height of sophistication and smart living, but cheese and tomato seemed very alien at that first encounter. The floppy white bread got stuck in a doughy lump at the top of my mouth and tasted of nothing in particular.

Eventually the stilettos came back, *tack, tack, tack*. As I followed Mrs Dixon-Child out of the station, I noticed how my friendly ticket inspector had put his footstool into his hut and locked the gate. He gave me a surreptitious little wave and I waved back.

It is amazing how much one comprehends without understanding a single spoken word. Mrs Dixon-Child had been late to meet the train because she couldn't find a parking space. She must have panicked and double-parked just to come and find me quickly. Illegal parking could incur a hefty fine, even though there were no yellow or red lines in 1959. As she manoeuvred the leather-upholstered Wolseley cautiously through the busy London streets, she explained all this to me – or something very much along those lines. Yet I didn't understand a single word of her chatter, despite the fact that I had learnt English for six years at school.

It was late afternoon. The amount of traffic around Victoria was quite overwhelming: several lanes of tailgating vehicles; revving engines; squealing brakes, and screeching tyres. It all appeared wonderfully strange and exciting to me. The cars had black number plates with white or silver lettering. There were no trams, no yellow buses, no cyclists as in Berlin, but mainly black cabs and nose-to-tail red double-decker buses. They were open at the rear on the kerbside, so that people could jump on and off in the slow-moving traffic. Long orderly queues of waiting commuters formed along the pavements. When a bus stopped, it looked as if it sucked the queue into its belly much like a long piece of well-oiled spaghetti – swiftly and smoothly without any pushing and shoving.

The air was thick with exhaust fumes; you couldn't see the other side of the wide streets clearly. All the buildings were of the same colour, charcoal black; there wasn't a single reddish brick in sight. An enormous number of chimney pots of varying sizes arose from the roofs, so that the skyline looked like the mouth of an old crocodile.[29]

The house at 12 Cranes Drive turned out to be quite different from the houses I had seen from the train. It was completely detached and stood on an attractive suburban road lined with large lime trees – and it had only one chimney. The outside walls consisted mainly of white panels between dark brown beams that reminded me a bit of Bavarian country houses, except that here the roof was quite small and perched on top of the house like a little hat rather than some meaningful protection.

My first thought was, 'I hope the cleaning lady does the windows,' because they were not only rather large but consisted of lots of little panels, each with four corners ready to collect dust and dirt. There were no lace curtains, just as there had been none at the windows of the British forces in Berlin; instead, there were heavy, velvety drapes

---

[29]   In 1956, the Clean Air Act started legally enforcing smokeless zones in London. Over the following decades, buildings had their stone facades cleaned bit by bit and restored to their original appearance.

on either side of each window, rather like the beautiful hangings I knew from medieval paintings.

A small black poodle greeted me like a long-lost friend, jumping up at me and yapping relentlessly until he was taken from the room with a *tut* and a sigh by Mrs Dixon-Child. The eight-year-old child stood in a corner of the room and eyed me suspiciously. She was a pretty, blonde little girl with a sullen face. She had had a long row of nannies, governesses and au pair girls, none of whom seemed to have stayed very long. The last one had left suddenly, just when Mrs Dixon-Child needed her most. That explained why I had been hired so quickly.

'Tomorrow, I have to go to London. Me go London all day, no Mrs Dixon-Child. You understand? *Tu comprends? Verstehen?*' Having realised that I didn't understand much of what she was saying, she was using huge gestures and 'pidgin foreign' and was shouting in order to get through to me. 'You make breakfast for Rosalind: give her food, cereal, milk, toast. Breakfast!'

I didn't know what cereals were, nor toast, for that matter. We ate things like salami or cheese on solid, dark rye bread for breakfast (with a knife and fork) and drank hot cups of herb tea.

'Now you go with Rosalind and buy ice-cream at the shop.' *Ice cream* and *shop* I understood. I also understood that she wanted to be left alone and that she had decided her daughter and I should get acquainted without being observed. I thought that was a very sensible idea.

Some coins were thrust into my hand with explicit directions as to the location of the shop. That, at least, was something we had practised at school repeatedly: how to give and receive directions in English.

As we left the house, I wanted to turn right as instructed but Rosalind stopped me and said she knew a short cut, a better way, and indicated the opposite direction. I thought, 'If we go her way I am completely at her mercy, because I don't know the layout of the roads, and she will order me around for the whole of my stay.'

I stood my ground, but so did she. In the end, I took off to the right without looking back, saying something like, 'See you at the shop.' I was taking an awful risk. What would I have done if the child hurt herself or disappeared? But I had the money, and I was pretty sure she wanted the ice cream and didn't want to upset her formidable mother.

Rosalind turned up at the shop at the same time as I did, and we smiled at each other with a hint of relief. On the way back, she came with me without any argument. She even allowed me to hold her hand whilst we were walking along the busy main road – she hardly seemed to notice because she was too busy licking her ice cream.

When we got back, her mother asked, 'All right? Any problems?'

Rosalind was watching me intently. 'Problems?' I queried, 'No, no, lovely ice cream, right money, thank you.'

In the evening, James Stewart walked through the door. I stared at him in disbelief. Rosalind jumped into her daddy's arms, wrapping her legs around his waist and her arms around his neck before he had even taken off his bowler hat.

Mr Dixon-Child looked exactly as James Stewart had done in the films from twenty years earlier. He was very calm, reserved but friendly. I doubt that he said more than ten sentences to me in all the months I lived with the family, which is perhaps not surprising as he was hardly ever at home.

He left the house before I got up in the mornings, or perhaps whilst I was getting up, because I often saw him walk down the road wearing his bowler hat and pin-stripe suit. He always held a briefcase in one hand and had a large newspaper tucked under his arm; the other hand operated a long, black umbrella like a walking stick. Identically dressed men joined him from other houses using the 'umbrella hand' to lift their bowlers elegantly an inch from their heads in greeting.

They were all catching the same train from Surbiton station into London. The car stayed in the garage and was used only for special outings, or for visits to Rosalind's grandparents at the weekend.

Mrs Dixon-Child was not like the typical married women of the time who stayed at home and looked after the family. She was clearly a modern woman with a mind and interests of her own.

On my first day, a car came to take her to the London ITV film studios. A whole week of rigorous filming was about to commence. I had to take Rosalind to school each morning after giving her breakfast. During the day I had to keep the dog company, do some light dusting and the washing up, and hand wash what Mrs Dixon-Child called her 'smalls'. Then I fetched Rosalind from school at half past three and organised afternoon tea for her and some of her friends.

It was an easy life; the only problem was handling these so-called 'smalls'. They were enormous! I had never seen anything like them and had no idea how to wash them. There were massive bras made from strong cloth that held their shape no matter what. Some continued in one piece down to the waist and were not only made of sturdy taffeta but also had metal structures and long flat bones in them. There were also armour-like, full-length corsets, huge suspenders and outlandish knickers, all to be washed in pure Fairy Snow, 'The Only Leading Powder that is Made of Real Soap' as it said on the packet. I never quite understood how Mrs Dixon-Child could let a stranger wash these things and then have them dry outside on a washing line where anyone might see them.

A couple of days after I arrived, Rosalind had friends for tea. Mrs Dixon-Child prepared most of the food the evening before, and I laid the table in the dining room as instructed. There were neatly cut sandwiches, cakes, and jellies and custard from Marks & Spencer. I made a fuss over Rosalind's friends to make them feel comfortable.

Everything went well until I casually pointed out that the sugar in the bowl on the table was all the sugar there was and asked the children 'to go easy' with it. Seconds later, Rosalind took the bowl and tipped all the sugar into her cup of hot tea so that the liquid spilt into the saucer, then onto the polished mahogany table and finally onto the parquet floor.

In the silence that followed, she looked back at me with triumphant defiance. I was standing right behind her. Without thinking or hesitating, I smacked her round the head just the way my mother would have done to me.

The friends gasped and Rosalind started to cry. 'I'll tell my mum,' she shouted, whilst pounding her feet on the floor in fury.

'Yes pleece, tell to parents,' I said, hoping to appear calm. Then I sent her to her room and locked her in.

I knew many lovely, noisy games to play with that age group – games loud enough to cover up Rosalind's shouting and banging at the door. For two whole hours I entertained the children as best I could and made them laugh and romp around all over the house and garden. I think they had a nice time, because they always liked coming back.

When it was time for them to go home, I unlocked Rosalind's door and told her to come and say goodbye. To my amazement she didn't sulk, as I would have done in her situation, but dried her tears and said goodbye nicely. Shortly afterwards Mrs Dixon-Child came home. Neither Rosalind nor I ever mentioned the incident to her. We got on very well for the rest of my stay, so much so that Mrs Dixon-Child sometimes gave us a puzzled look.

The Dixon-Childs were obviously rich – they even owned a television set. We watched BBC to see the popular *Black and White Minstrel Show*, a variety show with lavish costumes and American country songs. It was presented by white performers who had made their faces look black with make-up to complete the image of singing and dancing, happy-go-lucky slaves in harmonious, picturesque, rural settings. But I learned most of my English from TV advertisements, because usually we watched 'the other channel', ITV. Not one of the commercials in which Mrs Dixon-Child appeared was to be missed. 'It's on, it's on, do be quiet!' she would screech several times an evening, and then we would sit quiet as mice to watch 'her' advert.

Most commercials were about washing powders,[30] Camay soap and Gleem toothpaste, with a cute Golliwog advert for Robertson's Golden Shred Marmalade thrown in occasionally.[31] 'Daz White Knights are coming your way; big cash prizes.' Apparently, Mrs Flash was coming our way, too, with special rewards at the doorstep if you could prove you had some Flash in the house. I knew them all: nothing washed whiter than Persil, whereas OMO added brightness to cleanness and whiteness, and Tide promised the cleanest clean under the sun! I looked out for Mrs Dixon-Child's fair hair, painted lips, ample bosom and tightly corseted wasp waist on the small black-and-white screen, but I couldn't spot her. It took me quite some time to realise that it was only her hands that were being filmed. Whenever a woman held up a box of washing powder or toothpaste, nine times out of ten it was Mrs Dixon-Child's hands that were shown in close-up. Her main claim to fame was the long-running Fairy Liquid advert: 'Now hands that do dishes can feel soft as your face with mild green Fairy Liquid.' It was due to her glamorous 'hand career' that she needed someone to look after Rosalind and, ironically, someone to do all the tasks that involved getting her own hands wet or dirty.

Sometimes a big car from the film studios drew up and the driver was invited in for a coffee. On these occasions, Mrs Dixon-Child

---

[30] The term *soap opera* originated from radio and TV dramas being sponsored by soap manufacturers in the 1950s.

[31] I tried to look at this advert on YouTube to see why I thought it was cute at the time and found it had been 'removed for violating policy on hate speech'.

gave me extra money and told me to take the bus to Kingston and go to the cinema. 'Watch both movies, twice if you like, no need to hurry back.'

There were always A- and B-movies – the feature film and a less well-known film or documentary. They ran continuously all day long, so you could go into the auditorium at any time and watch for as long as you liked. I saw the *Carry On* films so often that my understanding of culture and language improved to the point where I began to appreciate why people laughed.

I always sat somewhere near the front, mainly because I was short-sighted but also to avoid the notorious 'single men in cinemas'. They never came to sit next to me and molest me – but the driver from the film studios did. I was in the kitchen, doing some last-minute ironing for Mrs Dixon-Child before leaving for the cinema. He came in for some more coffee and, as he passed me, firmly and unhurriedly grabbed my bum with both hands and gave it a good squeeze.

I was outraged. Did he think I was one of those Swedish au pairs who were renowned for sunbathing and swimming in the nude, and thus considered 'fair game'? I was speechless. Wolf-whistles from men on building sites were acceptable, but this?

Infuriated and offended, I hastened into the sitting room whilst the man was still in the kitchen. Mrs Dixon-Child was draped across the sofa with a cigarette holder in her beautiful hands. 'He touched me, here,' I spluttered indicating my bottom.

She seemed a little confused by this unexpected revelation and blunt approach, but she must have understood because that was the last time I was sent to the cinema by myself. There was obviously no longer a need for it.

I wrote to Schalli to say that I wasn't at my aunt's place in Brussels, that I had made it to England quite legally, and I would be staying until the autumn.

Some people believe the essence of who we are remains the same throughout life, but I am not so sure. When I wrote to inform Schalli that her seventeen-year-old daughter wasn't coming home but was now in a foreign country living with an unknown family, I thought nothing of it. Now I think that my behaviour was quite outrageous. I showed no empathy, no consideration of how my mother might feel.

Schalli handled it beautifully. Loving (but not gushing) letters arrived two or three times a week. I quite enjoyed writing back to her, normally after the television had closed down at eleven o'clock at night with a spirited rendering of the national anthem. She wrote that she would come to England to see for herself where I lived and to check that I was alright. I was sure this would never actually happen – or it was so far in the distant future that it wasn't worth worrying about.

# FIRST BOYFRIEND

## 1959

Mrs Dixon-Child introduced me to an au pair from Cologne who worked for a family across the road. Although neither of us were particularly keen to spend time with another German, she helped me a lot in finding my way around in the beginning.

On the very first weekend, we went together to the Continental Club in Kingston. The British were famous for their club culture, and we were told that this was a club for young people like us. The venue turned out to be in a large shed at the end of a shabby alleyway. We hesitated, but the music coming from the hut was compelling; it wasn't skiffle or jazz, but loud, throbbing rock 'n' roll – which in those days was seen as dangerous and subversive. Famously, Elvis only appeared on the Ed Sullivan television show from the waist up because his hip gyrations were considered too lewd.

The large room was packed, but not with English Teddy Boys or people from the continent (as the name of the club suggested). The hall was full of very tall, athletic-looking black men. Kingston, Jamaica had come to Kingston upon Thames. In retrospect, I wonder if they perhaps were the West Indian cricket team. We timidly made our way to an empty row of chairs lined up against one wall, hesitantly sat down and arranged our billowing petticoats and skirts.

Other than a single black man on the underground when I was nine years old, I had never seen any black people. I tried not to stare. The handsome young men looked at us occasionally, but nobody made a move to come and ask for a dance. My friend and I chatted to each other in what we hoped was a nonchalant, self-confident manner.

I noticed two young white men leaning against a little bar at the other end of the room. The taller one, with a Caesar haircut all combed forward as in Roman times, peeled himself away from the bar and ambled across the dance floor, aiming straight towards me. I was getting ready to stand up and accept his invitation to dance when, at the last second, he changed direction and stopped in front of my companion. I was left sitting by myself, feeling uncomfortable and somehow rejected, watching the young man jive competently with my acquaintance.

Years later, he told me he had done that on purpose to make me more interested in him. Perhaps it worked, because I remember being inordinately pleased when he asked me for the next dance.

'Come outside with me, I want to show you something,' he suggested, after we had danced together for a while.

I thought this young man was far too sure of himself and decided to show him how a decent German girl dealt with cheekiness. I had seen a film where a man took a girl outside and, when he tried to grab her and kiss her on the lips, she slapped him across the face. I was already constructing a suitably irate sentence in my mind to go with the intended action when the young man stopped and said, 'There you are. What do you think?'

He was pointing at a rickety old black car with spoked wheels that looked as if they had come off a pram or a little bicycle. 'I finished painting her this afternoon,' he added proudly.

The top of the car looked like a checkerboard of black-and-yellow squares, and there was a bright red line running all around the chassis. 'Do you want to come for a spin in her next Sunday?'

And so it was that I became acquainted with Brian Thompson, an eighteen-year-old printer's apprentice with a public-school education. I also became well acquainted with his car. Starting it up was quite a procedure, which normally involved cranking a starter handle.[32] The favourite and most successful method, however, was the push start – to which I was introduced on our first date.

The engine stalled in a quiet country lane. Brian skilfully applied what he called 'the foot brake' to bring the car to a final stop; this involved putting one foot through the rusted hole beneath the driver's seat and applying the sole of the shoe to the road surface. On the passenger's side there were also some holes through which you could see the road, but fortunately they were not big enough for a second 'foot brake'.

Influenced by tacky B-movies with car scenes of a provocative, flirtatious nature that started with young men pretending the car had broken down, once again I expected 'the worst'. Once again, I was proved wrong.

'Could you give us a push?' said Brian, grinning cheerfully at me.

It was raining. I was wearing my Sunday best: Schalli's kidskin gloves to hide my bitten fingernails; a light-coloured coat over a full skirt; nylon stockings, and delicate shoes with little pointed heels.

---

[32] A 'cranking handle' is a long metal bar bent at ninety degrees at two points. The driver inserted the crank handle through a hole at the bottom of the front grille and rotated it in a clockwise direction until the engine started.

Brian 1959, age 18

Why didn't I refuse? This wasn't how it was supposed to be; this didn't match the picture in my head. However, life's challenges help you discover who you are. Although I didn't want to get myself muddy and sweaty, it was of the utmost importance to me to be seen as a good sport. More than anything else, I wanted to fit in and be liked.

So, I pushed the wretched car. I scraped the dried mud off my shoes, legs, coat and face once we got to the pub in Esher where the Young Conservatives were meeting. The ladies' restroom was furnished with plush red armchairs and had long, spotless mirrors but, to my surprise, the toilets were of the same dreadful design as the Dixon-Childs': just a bowl half-full of water. I found it difficult to sit above this unsanitary arrangement for fear of being splashed from below. I learned in due course that all English toilets were like this, and that English people thought continental toilets with the dry shelf design were shocking and disgusting.

After I cleaned myself up, I joined the smartly turned-out gathering upstairs. All I remember is that people were standing around in small groups, sipping sherry and talking politely about things beyond my comprehension.

The English class system is a bit like the English lawn: it needs centuries of experience and careful tending. There is a story about an American asking an Englishman what the secret is for producing the much-admired, immaculate English lawn and being told, 'You only have to roll it and cut it regularly.'

'That's all?' the American asks.

'For six hundred years,' adds the Englishman.

To this day, I find the British class structure baffling. At home we had poor people and not-so-poor ones. People were not all the same: some were more intelligent than others, and everyone had individual qualities and backgrounds. But all children were educated together in state schools and there was no perception of different classes. Consequently, I didn't really appreciate the uniqueness of what Brian had to offer. One day we would attend a meeting of Young Conservatives in a posh part of Esher, the next we would be in a pub in the East End of London. Brian was in his third year of a six-year apprenticeship in a rough area near Tower Bridge and had learned to adapt his middle-class accent and refined ways to a Cockney lilt and more boisterous attitude when necessary.

He took me to the East End on one of our first dates. We entered a dingy-looking pub on the corner of a shabby, cobble-stoned lane.

The friendly, animated atmosphere inside was in stark contrast to the unprepossessing exterior – and to the sherry party I had endured with the Young Conservatives. It felt like the meeting of a large clan where everyone knew everyone else and made you feel welcome. You could help yourself to nibbles set out on the bar, not just peanuts and crisps but also roast potatoes and a variety of seafood.

Brian enquired about a small, round hole in one of the windows.

'Blimey, yeah! What a to-do tha' was! This 'ole in the winda is from a shootin' last weekend, but the blighta din't get 'is man.'

I managed to get the gist of that and was impressed by these outlandish goings-on. Just then the band on the small stage at the back started to play and Brian left me standing in the middle of the room to go and unpack his clarinet.

''Ere, ducky, come 'ere an' si' wiv us,' called a large, elderly lady as she lifted her pint glass invitingly towards me and made room on the bench. I squeezed between her and another woman, clutching my Bloody Mary and smiling reservedly.

A line of people had formed facing the stage and they were doing a jolly-looking sort of dance while bellowing, 'My ol' man said follow the van and don't dilly-dally on the way...' Some of the folks on the benches started swaying to the music and singing along. Soon the women on each side of me linked my arms to a raucous 'Maybe it's becoz I'm a Londoner...' Before long, everyone was joining arms and rocking side to side in exactly the same way as I had seen Bavarians do in their large beer tents. After an exhausting 'Knees up Mother Brown', the band took a well-deserved rest.

Where was Brian? I hadn't heard a clarinet nor seen him on the stage – but then, the air was so thick with smoke from cigarettes, pipes and cigars that it was difficult to make out anything with my short-sighted eyes. As I made my way to the dreaded toilets, I found him leaning against the bar.

'Top up?' he beamed at me happily. 'I'm going to be on next. They're going to play some jazz and they're letting me sit in on 'All of Me'.' He must have been gratified by the admiration in my eyes because he smiled at me affectionately.

I stood close to the stage and watched Brian with anticipation. His tall and handsome figure was reflected several times in the large mirrors strategically positioned for the strippers' performances. He licked his reed efficiently, gave the bandleader a nod and, when the drum and bass started, he began to play – only to be stopped after a couple of bars.

There was a hushed silence. The bandleader whispered, 'It's in F,' and gave the sign to start again, but Brian didn't play.

'I can only play in B-flat,' he said.

'Well, 'ow about 'Lady Be Good' in B-flat then?'

'I can only play 'All of Me' – it's the only tune I've practised so far,' he informed the bandleader, looking quite unflustered and unembarrassed.

'OK, tell you what, mate – practise 'All o' Me' in F and come back next week, o'right?'

When we went back a week later, Brian confidently played the theme tune in the required key and got a clap and a cheer from the audience. However, that was it; when the bandleader stepped back to give way to the customary clarinet solo with improvisations, Brian shook his head to indicate that he wasn't ready for such advanced artistry.

It takes many years to learn how to play jazz and improvise around a given theme.[33] Why didn't I take up an instrument and join in, instead of being satisfied with the eternal role of appreciative

---

[33]  I am pleased to add that Brian did achieve his goal and has become a very competent jazz musician.

MY LIFE IN CAPITALS

audience member? I guess it just wasn't the done thing for a woman, or I simply didn't have the creative urge.

We started visiting places like Humphrey Lyttelton's 100 club in Oxford Street, and the newly opened Ronnie Scott's club in Soho. On the few occasions that there was a woman on stage, it was a singer, not someone playing an instrument.

Brian's mother had no time for this 'negro music'. Being an accomplished concert pianist and cellist, she was of the opinion that anyone with a halfway decent classical training could easily extemporise on these primitive chord changes.

She lived in Winchester, where Brian took me for a weekend visit. Eliza Patricia Susanna Slingsby-Todd, known as Susan, seemed to me to be an old lady of at least sixty. Her full head of white hair was tinted a light shade of blue and framed her deeply lined but smiling face. She was actually forty-six at the time. Very tall, slim and strong

Susan 1962, age 49

boned, but with rather awkward movements, she looked and sounded like the archetypal headmistress of a girls' public school: part bossy, part jolly hockey sticks. She seemed incredibly English to me.

As Brian's car wasn't reliable enough for a long journey, we hitchhiked to Winchester. His mother greeted us warmly and showed us to a small bedroom with a double bed covered with scratchy-looking blankets firmly tucked under the mattress. The assumption that this seventeen-year-old girl, whom she had never met before, would find it normal to share a bed with her eighteen-year-old son was like a slap in the face. I didn't know how to protest nor, apparently, did Brian.

Shyness and the desire to fit in with local customs had its limits. Although I didn't dare demand to sleep on a sofa downstairs, I had to draw the line somewhere – and it was an imaginary one down the middle of the bed. My distress and embarrassment were complete when Susan appeared in the bedroom the next morning, carrying a tray of food and cheerfully enquiring if we had slept well. As I learned years later, apparently she had vowed that her sons should have every opportunity to sow a few wild oats and acquire the sort of knowledge that had been sadly lacking during her own strict Victorian upbringing.

I wonder if she would have felt the same if she had had any daughters; particularly in view of the fact that this was before 'the pill' was readily available and children born out of wedlock were called 'bastards'.

'And who is your favourite German philosopher, my dear?' Susan was making small talk whilst Brian was getting ready for a game of tennis with her. Plato was obviously the wrong answer. My mind froze and I was unable to give the name of any philosopher, German or not.

She tried to make it easier for me. 'Which German symphony do you like in particular?'

'The Ninth?' I sounded unsure. That was Beethoven, wasn't it? And he was German – or perhaps not? I wasn't at all clear about what was German and what wasn't. For years I took it for granted that Woolworth and C&A were German outlets simply because there were lots of them in Berlin.

I watched Susan and Brian play a forceful game of tennis with suitable admiration.[34] I had seen tennis courts in Berlin once or twice, but they were hard clay courts and only for the occupying armed forces. Susan and Brian played on a pristine grass court up on a hill, close to the picturesque village church in Littleton where Susan played the organ on Sundays.

When we returned, they had a little 'run through' of one of Schumann's 'Fantasiestücke' for clarinet and piano. 'Being German, you are surely familiar with this piece?' Susan asked me.

Fortunately, she didn't wait for a reply. At the time I couldn't distinguish between Schumann and Schubert; one was German, the other was Austrian, but which was which? Not that this would have been relevant to an English person. The difference between Germany and Austria is a bit like the difference between England and Scotland – for an outsider, it's all much the same.

Susan removed the roll-up cigarette that was stuck to her lips at all times – lit or unlit – and carefully unlocked her medium grand piano, which looked rather out of place in the little cottage. The instrument seemed to fill the whole living room. There was a brief piano introduction and off they went. Brian did his best, but he was struggling to transform the dots of the sheet music into beautiful sounds and found it hard to keep up with his mother's nimble fingers and musical expertise.

---

[34] Aged fourteen, Brian had made it to Junior Wimbledon.

I got up quietly and went to see Susan's husband, who was working in the garden. After her divorce from Brian's father, Susan had married a much older man who had worked for the railways and was now retired. 'Ave ya come ter give us 'n 'and, lass, or d'ya not like the racket iver an 'ave come ter escape?'

I liked him; he reminded me of the people in the pub in the East End of London. And I think he liked me – I was even under the impression that he flirted with me in a harmless, convivial sort of way. I was very surprised, therefore, when someone asked me at his funeral a few years later, 'How did you get on with old Desmond, then? It must have been difficult with him having been such a German-hater?' I had experienced nothing but kindness from Desmond, or was it a case of 'you see what you want to see'?

When Susan suggested a game of bridge in the afternoon, Desmond gave me a conspiratorial wink and anxious look as if to say he would be grateful if that activity could be sabotaged by some means. He needn't have worried. Not only did I not 'care for a quick rubber', but bridge wasn't a card game played outside Great Britain or the USA, so I didn't know it – yet! Instead, we played a simple card game for three people whilst Desmond sat contentedly in his well-worn wingback armchair, doing the crossword puzzle and smoking his pipe.

At the end of the weekend, Susan took us to the nearest A-road in her Morris Minor as a good starting point for thumbing a lift back to London and kissed me good-bye. This came as a bit of a surprise. There had been no kissing and hugging when we had arrived the day before – and why should there have been? And to my mind nothing much had changed since then to warrant this sudden intimacy.

'*Mmmmwah, mmmmwah,*' she went, gently touching her cheek to mine, first right then left, while pursing her lips in a French air kiss. Then our faces collided, and our lips briefly brushed against each other because I was going for a third one. I wasn't really used to

Schalli 1966, age 54

kissing anyone but my closest family, and then only by planting my lips resolutely on just one of their cheeks. Meeting some of Auntie Helga's friends in Brussels had, however, taught me the Belgian three-kiss rule (right cheek, left, then right again). Susan must have thought these young German girls really had no manners at all.

The etiquette of a culture you are not born into is one of the hardest things to learn. English etiquette is, in my opinion, particularly complicated; it is so obscure that the English language does not even have a proper word for it. [35]

When Schalli met Brian for the first time, she was far from impressed by his social graces. She came to England, as she had said she would, to check out the Dixon-Childs and see what I was

---

[35] The French have at least three expressions that instantly spring to mind: etiquette, décorum, bienséance.

doing. They received her courteously for afternoon tea and passed the 'concerned-mother test', but I didn't feel too thrilled with Schalli interfering in my new independent life. Nonetheless, I went with her for a week's holiday to Cornwall, which was part of the teachers' exchange programme she had used to make the journey to England.

The summer of 1959 was particularly long and hot. Carbis Bay, near St Ives, looked and felt like an Italian holiday resort with its huge sandy beach and picturesque cottages along the hilltops. Brian decided he would give me a surprise and turned up at the bed and breakfast where I was sharing a room with Schalli. He had borrowed a decrepit old tent and groundsheet and had hitchhiked to Cornwall.

When this unwashed young man with a beaming smile and filthy backpack arrived, I tried to explain to Schalli who he was. He stood in our pristine little bedroom, looking and smelling utterly out of place, rather like a soldier straight from the battlefield. As I introduced him, he decided he couldn't greet my mother whilst burdened with all that cumbersome baggage. He sat down on the nearest bed, removed the straps of the heavy backpack, slipped out of the harness and got up with a sigh of relief.

Schalli never ceased to enjoy telling the story with a shudder of horror. 'This grubby young man simply sat down on *my* bed, which was covered with a snow-white, silk bedspread. He was carrying a huge rucksack on his back plastered in mud and worse from half the fields of England. As he removed it and dropped it, the rusty hooks and buckles got entangled in the delicate lace of the bedspread. Utterly unaware of his offensive behaviour, he then proceeded to grab my hand and shake it heartily without even waiting for it to be proffered.'

He came across as an uneducated oaf who didn't even have the decency to wait for a lady – and an older person, at that – to extend her hand first. That was something even an infant would know, according to Schalli.

Before my mother went back to Berlin, Brian took us for a proper English cream tea at a smart hotel in London. It was somewhere in Knightsbridge, close to Harrods. Schalli didn't say anything at the time, but she was convinced we would either be barred from the hotel or thrown out because Brian was wearing old jeans and a T-shirt instead of a conventional suit and tie.

She was reluctant to get into the black-and-yellow chequered car, and I didn't blame her! She was assuming that the old wreck would be parked discreetly somewhere out of sight. Brian, however, stopped directly in front of the imposing hotel entrance, diligently helped her out, then handed the car over to the valet to park it after warning him about the dangerous hole in the floor.

A door attendant, wearing a top hat and white gloves, was standing in front of the double doors leading to the entrance hall. He bowed, bade us welcome and held open the heavy doors. We stepped into a magnificent foyer adorned with palm trees. Schalli stopped, adjusted her hat and surreptitiously inspected her cotton gloves, which were slightly soiled after the car ride, whilst Brian went to the reception desk. The concierge showed us to the lift and asked the liftboy to take us to the penthouse café on the top floor. So far so good.

'Good afternoon, sir. Table for three?' purred the headwaiter. 'May I take the name?'

'Oh, we haven't booked a table,' came Brian's reply.

Schalli blanched; this was it, now we would be asked to leave. But far from it. We ended up at the best table by the window. Neither Schalli – nor I, for that matter    could understand why he was being treated so courteously. It felt as if some sort of magic was being performed, and in a way it was. The public-school accent and the nonchalant, confident attitude did the trick. Besides, the staff were probably used to dealing with the eccentricities of some of their 'better' customers and their offspring. Schalli's oft-repeated dictum that you will be treated according to how you are dressed was proven wrong, at least on this occasion. Always willing to learn and open to modern ideas, she embarked on a lifelong love of what she called 'the English laissez-faire'.

We had a sumptuous feast not only of scones, clotted cream and jam, but also delicately- cut cucumber sandwiches and fancy cupcakes. Nobody commented on the divergence in table manners, but I noticed that Brian kept one hand in his lap whereas Schalli and I carefully kept both hands on the table, each according to their upbringing. At the end, the bill was automatically handed to Brian. Schalli objected in vain; he insisted on paying, although I knew he had no money. It probably set him back half a month's apprenticeship earnings.

Schalli had brought her 8mm film camera and filmed the popular sights and the street life: red double-decker buses (in black and white), London taxis, bobbies on the beat, and orderly queues of multinational-looking people. We went into Downing Street (it wasn't fenced off in those days) and filmed Schalli going up to the bobby who was standing in front of Number 10. The façade had just been cleaned and restored to its original, natural yellow-brick appearance.[36]

Schalli filmed hula hoops, Barbie dolls and signs saying, 'No Dogs, No Blacks, No Irish'. Even the Dixon-Childs were filmed, but of Brian and me there is only one blurred long-distance shot as we frolicked around in the sea in Cornwall. She obviously didn't envisage that this strange young man would play a major role in my life and become the father of her grandchildren.

In October 1959, I left England with a heavy heart to start my physiotherapy training in Berlin. I had come to England in search of adventure and that feeling of lightness I had experienced in Brussels,

---

[36]    The smog-derived black colour of the façade at 10 Downing Street was considered so iconic that the cleaned-up bricks were later painted black to preserve the image.

that sensation of being a snail not carrying its shell. I had found it, and much more besides. We would write, of course, and Brian would come to see me in Berlin, or we would meet at some place in the middle – and I would definitely come back to England soon.

Astrid 1960, age 18

# PHYSIOTHERAPY

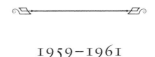

## 1959–1961

Happiness is not a goal, it is a by-product. It's not something we achieve but rather a side-effect of meaningful, fulfilling activity that makes us focus on the present.

I was happy during the intense, action-packed two years of physiotherapy training that followed my return from England in 1959. Mornings were spent at various hospitals and clinics, in the afternoons we had lectures, and in the evenings, I worked as an usherette in the British NAAFI cinema. Weekends were taken up with studying and intensive socialising, which included all-night parties with skinny-dipping at sunrise. According to Schalli, I was hardly ever at home. She writes, *Astrid appears to be driven. It is as if she feels she is missing out on something important if she is not constantly out and about.*

I loved learning all the practical stuff like gymnastics, yoga, meditation, special types of massage and various therapies involving water, light, air, heat and cold. Theoretical subjects like anatomy and physiology were backed up by observing operations. Standing amongst the surgeons, nurses and anaesthetists around the operating table, I felt utterly out of place yet privileged and important.

The main thing was not to faint, and I never did. The patient was completely covered with only the body part to be operated on visible. The first incision looked as if the scalpel was cutting into fondant icing, not a person's skin and flesh. There was always friendly, casual chatter alongside the surgeon's commands and nurses' announcements.

I remember one occasion when the weekend was being discussed. 'Yes, we had a lovely time sailing – more suction here, please – plenty of wind for once – watch what you're doing, clamp here, quickly – Anna had made something called a walnut salad, absolutely delicious – swab – itchy nose, my left.' A nurse lifted the surgeon's mask for a second and scratched his nose for him.

On another occasion, the anaesthetist whispered to me, 'I have to go and point Percy at the porcelain.' He handed me a black rubber ball with deep folds. 'Give this a squeeze every now and then – back in a sec.'

We were all dressed the same, covered in white from top to toe with only our eyes showing. He had no idea who I was, and most likely had never heard of a physiotherapist as it was a new profession; he probably assumed I was a nurse or an experienced medical student. After a while I squeezed the ball, wondering what this was all about. Then I realised that the patient's chest rose every time I squeezed the ball and I started to panic. How often and how strongly should I do it? What did he mean by 'every now and then'? I decided to do it to my own breathing rhythm, which was probably much too fast. The anaesthetist doubtless came back quite quickly but it seemed like an eternity to me. Luckily, he didn't seem to find anything amiss.

Meeting the patient in the ward the next morning was always a somewhat mystical, almost spiritual, experience. Less than twenty-four hours earlier, this person's body had lain inert on a slab with his entire small intestine (all twenty-two feet of it) heaped on the table. I had looked into the empty abdominal cavity and seen the lumbar spine from the inside; I had kept him breathing with my hands on the rubber ball; I had witnessed how the guts were unceremoniously stuffed back into the cavity to settle into their preferred position by themselves. And here was that same body, the same person, having a cup of tea and speaking to me quite normally.

'They say the operation went very well. They are going to do another small procedure this afternoon to make it even better.' I just smiled, nodded my head and continued with the post-operative ventilating routine. I had been at the emergency meeting regarding this patient and had seen the X-ray with the missing pair of scissors in his stomach. There were regular mishaps – although they were usually not quite that appalling. I learnt a lot, not only about the human body and mind but also about human nature and human fallibility.

A few visits to the morgue were deemed beneficial for a deeper grasp of anatomy. Only two or three of us went at a time. On my first visit, a pathologist was already conducting a dissection in the middle of the otherwise empty autopsy room. An attendant announced, 'Here are the young ladies from the physio-school.'

The pathologist put down the rib-cutter, looked up, took a deep breath and sighed. He threw a cover over parts of the pale, naked body in front of him and waved to us to come closer and stand right next to the corpse with the caved-in chest. My friend grabbed my hand and then asked for a chair.

The pathologist did his best to keep us focussed on the educational purpose of the visit by talking non-stop and asking us questions. 'We are looking for a thrombus in the brain or the heart. I just checked the pulmonary artery – negative. What do you call an embolism in the brain? After I finish removing the top of the skull, what part of the brain will you see? What is the Latin name for the posterior structure, and what is its function?' The term *autopsy* derives from Ancient Greek 'to see for oneself', and we definitely saw and experienced the human body in a way that sketches and diagrams could never convey.

Some of my colleagues left early or refused a second visit, but I managed to stay focussed by listening to the pathologist as I watched the post-mortem procedures. I was rather pleased with myself for being a tough cookie. It wasn't until I was passing a butcher's shop a couple of days later, where whole sides of pork and other animal parts were displayed, that I suddenly had to throw up on the pavement without any apparent reason. For years afterwards, I found it difficult to go into a butcher's shop.

Deferred reaction? Yes, of course. Emotions are often not what they appear to be. There is no running away from our innate reactions; if we try to sweep strong feelings under the carpet, they tend to explode somewhere else – often in disguise and not as obvious as in the case of my autopsy and butcher's shop experience.

One interesting side-effect of learning about the human body and mind was perpetual hypochondria. I think all the students experienced this. No matter what disorder we studied, I started to suffer from some of the symptoms. The powers of suggestion are very strong. If my hands so much as shook when reaching for a cup of tea, I interpreted it as a warning sign for Parkinson's; the slightest headache or neck stiffness was an indication of the onset of cervical spondylosis; when we studied the symptoms of meningitis, I not only had the stiff neck and headache but also became over-sensitive to light and loud noise. I was about to go down with meningitis until we started studying another condition with different symptoms.

We were taught by devoted idealists and enthusiasts who were instrumental in creating the new profession of physiotherapy. They felt that there should be someone apart from nurses and doctors, someone with enough time to listen to the patients and give hands-on help and advice before, during and after a hospital stay.

Only a small number of staff – and practically none of the patients – really knew who we were and what we were doing on the wards. As I passed through, wearing my white coat and Bertelmann's wooden health sandals, patients often called out 'Nurse, nurse, I need the bedpan' or 'Can I have a cup of coffee?' or 'Nurse, please adjust my sandbags'. Pointing out that I wasn't a nurse, that I wasn't wearing the nurses' head gear, didn't make much difference. Sometimes I obliged, but Matron didn't like me messing around in the sluice fetching bedpans. That was a job for a trainee nurse.

The men's wards were much more fun than the women's. The men coped better with their situation – or at least that is how it seemed to me at the time. They would heckle each other and try to tease me.

'Mr Valentin's sandbag has slipped. He has been calling for a nurse for ages and is in agony. He's over there, in the bed by the window.'

The old man looked at me hopefully as I approached. 'So, where is the sandbag then?' I asked, trying to sound all business-like and professional. Medical sandbags of different sizes were being used to support and prop up limbs and joints to keep them in an optimal position; it was going to be part of my job to suggest where and how to apply them.

Mr Valentin threw back his bedcover and pointed to his bare crotch. I hadn't yet come across any testicular and scrotal surgery and didn't realise that a small sandbag supporting the testes was crucial after such an operation. Nonetheless, I nonchalantly lifted his two shaven orbs into my hands and arranged them carefully on the repositioned sandbag. I had to repeat the performance every morning from then on, much to the amusement of the whole ward. Of course, I knew that Mr Valentin pushed the bag out of position when he saw me coming, but the little performance gave everyone so much pleasure that I played along with it.

During the evenings, I was subjected to an entirely different environment. The pay at the NAAFI cinema was very good and there wasn't much to do. After the soldiers had bought their tickets and sweets (mainly Maltesers), I had to show them to their seats and make sure that the no-smoking signs were obeyed. In Great Britain smoking was still permitted in cinemas.

'Pleeze don't smoke. Pleeze put your cigarette out. Smoking is not allowed,' I would beg.

When the offending lad replied with a mouth-load of abuse, accompanied by expressive gestures, his comrades would come to my assistance: 'Oh come on, cool it, mate. Cut the little Fräulein some slack, she's only doing her job.'

That always worked even when no Royal Military Police, or 'Redcaps' as they were known, were in the audience. The RMP were incredibly strict and took law enforcement very seriously in Berlin, with the result that the British soldiers had a very good reputation and knew that they had to be on their best behaviour the moment they stepped outside the barracks.

I had to stay in the auditorium throughout the film show and control the sound levels from a little desk in the back of the room, which also had a panic button in case of disorderly behaviour. There was never any cause to use it. I saw every film at least five times; the sentimental songs in *South Pacific* will stay ingrained in my brain for eternity, together with the musty smell of the cinema jam-packed with young men in uniform.

Civilians were not officially allowed in, but when Brian came to visit me in Berlin, I smuggled him in. I think he felt a bit uncomfortable amongst all the soldiers because he had no experience of army life; born in 1940, he was in the first age group that was no longer conscripted.

I met up with Brian several times during those two years; we met in Cologne, I went to see him in England one Easter holiday, and he came to Berlin twice. After I passed my physiotherapy exam in the autumn of 1961, I felt I deserved a little break and went to visit him again. I thought I'd just have a few months off before starting the compulsory year in a hospital in Berlin. But – as I was about to find out – the best-laid plans of mice and men oft go astray.

# LEAVING BERLIN

## 1961

The infamous Berlin Wall was built in 1961. That was the year I finished my physiotherapy training and left Berlin to spend a few months with Brian in London. With the erection of the Wall, the communist East German authorities finally put a stop to 250,000 East Berliners crossing into the West each day to go to work there. They also put a stop to East Germans 'voting with their feet' by leaving communist Germany altogether. More than 3,500,000 people had emigrated to the West via the West Berlin loophole within twelve years – an intolerable brain drain and reduction of manpower for the GDR. Now the divided city, with two widely divergent political systems and two different currencies, was totally segregated and would remain so for the next twenty-eight years.

Our cleaning lady, who lived in the East, was a *Grenzgänger*, a cross-border commuter. That is what we called the people who came across the border to earn Westmarks, which were worth at least four times the amount of Eastmarks. Mrs Thun, whom we had nicknamed *Thunfisch*, came to us once a week and had become part of our little family over the years. She never took her hard-earned Westmarks with her across the border but left them with Schalli for safe-keeping – just in case, for an emergency. Her big mouth might easily get her into trouble with the East German Secret Police, she thought, and she might therefore have to flee to the West one day as she had no wish to end up in Siberia as a political prisoner.

She also kept a bag of basic necessities at our flat. As it turned out, she never had to make use of that, nor did she ever take possession of her accumulated money. The Wall was built practically overnight, and there was no time for making any arrangements. A quick telephone call was not possible because the wires between East and West Berlin had been cut nine years before (in 1952). Letters and parcels were opened and searched, and they would take far too long to arrive – and were often incomplete. So, from one day to the next, Thunfisch was unable to come to us nor contact us.

She had worked for us for ten years without taking payment – for nothing. There was no way of getting the money to her after the Wall was built. Schalli eventually managed to contact Thunfisch's daughter, who lived in West Germany, and she took charge of her mother's nest egg. Perhaps she managed to pass some of it on to her mother three decades later when the Wall finally came down and families were reunited.

Although I felt sorry for Thunfisch and sad that I would never see her again, the news reports about the border troubles didn't particularly interest me. I was far too preoccupied with myself. I was sorting through my belongings and clearing my wardrobe and desk. I would serve my obligatory practical year in Hamburg when I returned from London, so I wouldn't be coming back to this flat in Spandau.

Gerd and Schalli filmed me packing an overnight bag and defiantly smoking a cigarette in the living room as we had our last cup of coffee together. You can't see much on the black-and-white film, but

I recognise the flat and the flowery wallpaper in my bedroom. I used to stare at that wallpaper for hours when I was sick, tracking the little rosebuds on it. They repeated in a pattern that resembled the knight's moves in a game of chess and provided hours of 'entertainment'.

I had lived in that flat on Kemmannweg for seven long teenage years. It was home and has always remained home in my heart, despite the fact that I was so eager to leave it. It is the same flat that my children know from their frequent visits to Berlin. It is the flat where Schalli lived all by herself for another forty-four years, until she died in 2005 aged ninety-three.

Because of the erection of the Wall, I had to fly from Tempelhof to Heathrow. It was my very first flight and it took over four hours. The propeller-driven aircraft was so slow that it reacted quite dramatically to air pockets. Every now and then for a few seconds it felt like being on a roller coaster or an out-of-control lift plummeting to the ground. I remember the sensation of my body leaving the seat and being held back by the safety belt as loose objects took grotesque flight paths through the cabin. People were asked to extinguish their cigarettes during air turbulence, and the gorgeous-looking young stewardesses tended not to serve liquids unless there was a particularly settled stretch of flying.

Brian collected me from the airport with his motorbike, so it was a good thing that I had travelled light and come with only an overnight bag. After a half-hearted attempt to find some bedsit accommodation, I moved into the flat Brian shared with his friend, Bob. It was a loft conversion in a private house in Putney and consisted of a kitchen, a bathroom, one room for Bob and one for Brian and me; the little kitchen doubled as the living room.

Brian was still a printer's apprentice and earned very little money, so I started looking for work straight away. The British Physiotherapy Board had accepted my German exam; I had a certificate stating that

I was allowed to practise in the UK, but I didn't have a work permit. You could only obtain that from outside the country, not when you were already in the country on a visitor's visa.

The Indian dentist in Lower Richmond Road didn't seem to mind about work permits. He employed me as his dental assistant, telephonist, receptionist, secretary and cleaning lady for six pounds a week. That wasn't great, but it was a reasonable salary. There were just the two of us; he looked after the work to be done in people's mouths and I did everything else. There was also a dental technician, but his domain was at the rear of the house facing the back garden.

The fact that I had no training as a dental nurse didn't seem to bother the Indian dentist. He showed me which utensils to use for mixing the amalgam and roughly how much mercury to apply to make it nice and smooth. If it was too soft, the filling would fall out after a couple of days; if it was too thick, he couldn't work with it, and I had to re-mix it. He mixed some of the more complicated pastes himself whilst I used the time to attend to 'front of house' duties, receiving the next patient in the waiting room or bringing the appointment ledger up to date.

When there were no patients the dentist would sit in a corner of the surgery, smoke his pipe and do nothing – while I cleared away the utensils, sterilised the implements by boiling them, filled in and filed the records, wiped the cupboards and dental chair, and cleaned the floor and windows.

His English was not much better than mine and he had a very strong accent. I found it difficult to understand anything he said – and he probably had the same problem with me – yet we communicated quite satisfactorily about the work to be done. When the little doorbell tinkled in the waiting room to announce the arrival of the next patient, he would gesticulate towards the window, indicating that I should open it, extinguish his pipe and spray a liberal amount of mint freshener into his mouth – with little success, I hasten to add, because the room stank of old tobacco fumes and his breath was disgusting.

When the telephone rang, we used to look at each other fearfully. Who would have the nerve to answer it? Using the telephone is by far the most difficult thing to do in a foreign language, which shows how much we rely on body language, facial expressions and lip reading to communicate. And when the person on the other end of the line is very angry and in pain, it makes conversing with them even more difficult.

Sometimes the patients didn't bother to ring but came in person to present the filling that had fallen out or show an angry swelling around a clicking jaw. Nervousness that wasn't quite guilt (though it came close to it) would come over me. I knew that we had broken this person's jaw during the extraction of a lower molar the previous day; I had felt the little snap whilst supporting and holding the chin.

'Oh, dearie me,' was all the dentist would say to the complaining patient. Then he would hand over a box of painkillers and antibiotics, of which he had an ample supply in his drawer.

There was an outside toilet; to get to it, you had to go down a narrow, dark corridor, through the dental technician's room and out through a rickety door into the garden. The dental technician sat amongst his plaster casts, false teeth and gums strewn over the raised work bench by the dirty window and waved to me as I passed through. The toilet was really part of his room, just a corner partitioned off with some plasterboard, but it could only be reached from the garden. It was therefore not surprising that the dental technician was the first person to guess I was pregnant. 'You've been throwing up again. Have you seen a doctor yet?'

I felt comfortable having him speak to me like that because we had made friends during my frequent trips through his room. I had been allowed to touch his hair, which felt much softer than I had expected, and he had explained in detail how much trouble it is to cut a black man's hair to make it look like a smooth halo.

I went to the doctor. They took a blood sample, and I was told to telephone a few days later to find out the result. There were no quick pregnancy tests or a morning-after pill in those days. Even 'the pill' was not available. You only slept with someone you were prepared to marry and who, you thought, would want to marry you. Call it love, if you like.

I went to the red phone box at the bottom of Dryburgh Road, where we lived, and anxiously followed the instructions about how to operate the A and B buttons. I was nervous, not only because of the result I was about to find out, but of having to speak to someone in English without seeing him or her.

My worst fears came true: I didn't understand what the woman at the other end was saying. She wasn't telling me whether I was pregnant or not. I persevered: 'Positive? Pleeze to tell me what it means.' As far as I was concerned, 'positive' could mean 'It's OK, you are off the hook'.

But I was firmly, and happily, 'on the hook'. After a moment of dumbstruck astonishment that my body was actually able to perform such a miracle, I started feeling extremely pleased and excited. So was Brian.

He made plans for the wedding. It had to be soon, because the financial year was about to finish, and we could get a whole year's tax rebate worth a hundred pounds or so if we could get into the Wandsworth Register Office before the 6th of April. We did – 31st March 1962 at 7.50 in the morning. Brian had managed to persuade them to put in an extra slot before the normal eight o'clock opening.

I started writing a letter to Schalli to tell her about the new situation. After she died, I found this letter amongst the few possessions she had kept. It is eleven pages long, written on narrow-lined blue airmail paper and was composed over several days. Every lunchtime I sat down at my little desk in the dentist's waiting room and continued writing. It goes on and on about all sorts of trivia, and only comes to the point on the very last page. But then the announcement that I am expecting a baby and am getting married in three weeks' time is virtually glowing with happiness and proud anticipation.

I wasn't there to see my mother's reaction. All I know is that, throughout the twenty-five years of my marriage, she got on well with Brian. She was a wonderful grandmother to my three children, and she turned out to be my closest friend and ally.

The restlessness that had driven me throughout my teenage years left me. I felt I had arrived. I would live in an 'exotic' place, far away from Germany and boring normality. Vows had been made, the future was assured, I was in love, and I was loved.

With the marriage came British citizenship; that meant that I could now work as a physiotherapist in the local hospital and earn some decent money. Brian was in his sixth and final year of apprenticeship and would soon earn enough to keep us. I, of course, would have to stay at home with the baby.

As I couldn't have a big wedding day, wafting down the aisle in a meringue-style wedding dress, just to be contrary I wanted the opposite – but it would have to be something to make the day special and outrageous. We decided we would roar up to the register office on the motorbike, dressed in jeans, bomber jackets and helmets. We would grab two random people off the street to be our witnesses, and afterwards we would get back on the bike and speed off to the coast, just the two of us. Any destination would do, as long as it satisfied my romantic vision and chimed with the feeling you get at the end of a Western where John Wayne rides off into the sunset.

It was a great plan and, because I so wish it had happened that way, I confess that I have occasionally told people that fictitious version of my wedding day and pretended it really took place. But alas, that account does not correspond with the truth, as evidenced by this wedding photo.

When Brian's father got wind of the impending nuptials, he decided it would be sacrilege and a disgrace to the family not to mark the event in some conventionally acceptable manner. Ignoring our wishes, he organised the family (including everyone from both his first and his second marriages) to turn up at 7.30am outside the register office – with the instruction to dress down.

Brian and Astrid on their wedding day outside the register office

MY LIFE IN CAPITALS

Brian and I borrowed a coat each. Our landlady lent me her fur hat; apparently under no circumstances could the bride appear with an uncovered head. I managed to find one of Schalli's smart leather gloves in the back of the wardrobe – unfortunately, just the one, but that would have to do. And I bought a lovely pair of high-heeled shoes from Dolcis on Putney High Street, with money we didn't really have.

Nowadays I wouldn't embark on such a significant occasion without some preparation, but not then. All I knew was that you had to repeat the vows as prompted by the registrar and that the phrases would be in fragments of a manageable size. I also knew that the wedding ring would be on the left hand, not the right hand as is customary in Germany. What could possibly go wrong?

I felt very important and euphoric. I was centre stage in a way I had never been before. My heart was pounding as I started repeating the words loudly – but perhaps not so clearly – in front of Brian's relatives, a gathering of about fifteen people.

'For better or for worse / till death do us part.' These were very serious vows. I concentrated and tried to really mean every word of it.

'That I know not of any lawful impediment', continued the registrar and my mind started racing: 'impediment'? It wasn't a word I had heard before! What did it mean?

Yet I dutifully continued repeating the words until I got to 'why I, Astrid Schade, may not be joined in matrimony…' I stopped. 'Matrimony'? Another word I had never heard before! I could not continue; I had to know. So, with a sudden flash of audacity, I blurted my question out loud, 'What does matrimony mean?'

There was a slight gasp; the room itself seemed to stiffen and hold its breath.

'Just repeat after me,' the registrar snapped with some irritation.

'I can't promise something I don't understand,' I persisted stubbornly. 'It wouldn't count.'

The registrar waved both arms like a conductor and spluttered, 'Matrimony! Matrimony! It's what you are doing here!'

'Marriage, wedding,' Brian intervened, pointing at me and at himself – back and forward – and then waving the wedding ring under my nose.

As is often the case, my impetuous action left me feeling somewhat foolish and self-conscious. I gave in and repeated the phrase like a good girl. The incident was not discussed on the day – at least not in front of me – but it was most certainly mentioned on many occasions later on and became a bit of a family joke.

Brian's father had insisted on a short reception at his house in Walton-on-Thames, where some friends and neighbours joined the gathering. For me that was excruciatingly embarrassing. I had to make polite conversation with people I had never met before, who felt obliged to give me presents – silver teaspoons, second-hand towels and plastic flowers. We couldn't get away quickly enough.

Our flatmate, Bob, who was one of our witnesses, kindly took us back to Putney in his car as soon as it was acceptable to leave. There we changed into our jeans and T-shirts, jumped onto Brian's motorbike and went to see *Ben Hur*, a Hollywood epic that lasted four hours. We had wanted to see it for a long time, but it was only shown on Saturdays when we were normally at work. After that, we treated ourselves to a meal in one of the Chinese restaurants that were springing up everywhere and then went back to the flat.

Finding a place to live wasn't easy. In the papers there were quite a few adverts for affordable flats to rent, and we spent every Sunday looking at possibilities, but the doors would close as soon as we said that we were expecting a baby. The notices in the windows that read 'No Dogs. No Blacks. No Irish' should have also said 'No Expectant Mothers. No Babies'.

After several weeks of fruitless searching, our hopes were raised when we went to see a flat in Tooting and found that there was no sign in the window. The lady who opened the door was obviously pregnant. Mrs Cirago was Italian and was expecting her fourth baby. No, no it was *no problema* at all that we were expecting a little addition to the family.

We moved into a flat that consisted of a kitchen and one other room, which served as living room and bedroom. It had an independent entrance at the back of the house, where Brian could also park his motorbike safely next to our outside toilet. It was perfect. Mrs Cirago was only too happy to give me advice, old nappies and baby clothes, and we ended up having our babies within a couple of weeks of each other.

The closest hospital was St Stephen's in Chelsea. Brian took me there in a taxi after my waters broke. It was early in the morning. At first, the Jamaican nurse at the reception desk wasn't at all welcoming. 'Please come back in the afternoon. Visiting hours are from two o'clock to four o'clock.' I really didn't look big enough to be about to give birth and it took a while for Brian to convince her that I was having contractions every three minutes.

It still took another few hours before the Irish midwife declared, 'It's a boy,' – long enough for Brian to start smoking again. After hours of stressful yet uneventful waiting, he was a nervous wreck. Without thinking, he accepted a cigarette from another anxious, expectant father who was waiting with him. In those days men weren't allowed anywhere near the birthing room until it was all over. Brian had actually given up smoking seven months earlier because the cigarette smoke had made me feel nauseous. Now he went and bought several packets and proceeded to chain-smoke in the corridor until Erik was born. He was called in, once the little bundle of new life had been washed, weighed and dressed, but he couldn't come upstairs to the ward with me because visiting time was over.

Astrid and baby Erik 19.10.1962

I found this picture in Schalli's photo album. She liked to tell the story of how she had shown this photo of her daughter to a colleague and how this colleague had thought it was of a schoolgirl playing with a doll. 'Isn't she a bit old to be playing with dolls?' she remarked. But this picture was taken at a party on my twenty-first birthday with baby Erik, who was three weeks old. So, I was twenty years old when I got married, became a mother and settled down in England.

It never ceases to amaze me that the dirty, hungry little girl scratching for edible weeds in the rubble of post-war Berlin somehow ended up only fifteen years later as a respectable British citizen, an adult with a family, and eventually with a house, a garden and enough food to feed an army.